The Sound of Nonsense

'There's no sense like nonsense, and here's a no-nonsense survey of it, from the simply silly to the profoundly pointed – a guide to the art of nonsense across cultural levels, at once scholarly and entertaining, original and enlightening.'

PAUL DUTTON, *Writer and Oral Sound Artist, Canada*

'Richard Elliott's *The Sound of Nonsense* is an exhilarating, well-informed, and very well-written book. Elliott shows an easy familiarity with sources in many languages, including Russian. His principal theoretical assertion is that nonsense occurs in the moment "when sense-making is forced into code-switching"; he also offers the suggestion that nonsense as such supports sociality. Although the book appears to be principally about popular culture, it works closely with sound poetry and with recent experimental styles in modern vocal performance, revealing how they blend with the "popular" forms. It is a work that is rewarding not only for its ideas, but for its searching analysis of individual songs and unusual word-sound combinations. A satisfying book.'

IRVING MASSEY, *Emeritus Professor of English and Comparative Literature, University at Buffalo, USA*

THE STUDY OF SOUND

Editor: Michael Bull

Each book in The Study of Sound offers a concise look at a single concept within the field of sound studies. With an emphasis on the interdisciplinary nature of the topics at hand, the series explores a range of core issues, debates, and objects within sound studies from a variety of perspectives and within a multitude of contexts.

Editorial Board:

Carolyn Birdsall, Assistant Professor of Television and Cross-Media Culture, University of Amsterdam, The Netherlands

Martin Daughtry, Assistant Professor of Music, Arts and Humanities, NYU, USA

Michael Heller, Associate Professor, Department of Music, University of Pittsburgh, USA

Brian Kane, Associate Professor, Department of Music, Yale University, USA

Marie Thompson, Lecturer, School of Film and Media, University of Lincoln, UK

James Mansell, Assistant Professor of Cultural Studies, Department of Culture, Film and Media, University of Nottingham, UK

Forthcoming Titles:

Sirens by Michael Bull
Sonic Intimacy by Malcolm James
Humming by Suk-Jun Kim
Sonic Fiction by Holger Schulze

The Sound of Nonsense

Richard Elliott

Bloomsbury Academic
An imprint of Bloomsbury Publishing Inc

B L O O M S B U R Y
NEW YORK · LONDON · OXFORD · NEW DELHI · SYDNEY

Bloomsbury Academic
An imprint of Bloomsbury Publishing Inc

1385 Broadway 50 Bedford Square
New York London
NY 10018 WC1B 3DP
USA UK

www.bloomsbury.com

**BLOOMSBURY and the Diana logo are trademarks
of Bloomsbury Publishing Plc**

First published 2018

© Richard Elliott, 2018

All rights reserved. No part of this publication may be reproduced or transmitted in any form or by any means, electronic or mechanical, including photocopying, recording, or any information storage or retrieval system, without prior permission in writing from the publishers.

No responsibility for loss caused to any individual or organization acting on or refraining from action as a result of the material in this publication can be accepted by Bloomsbury or the author.

Library of Congress Cataloging-in-Publication Data
A catalog record for this book is available from the Library of Congress.

ISBN: HB: 978-1-5013-2455-0
PB: 978-1-5013-2454-3
ePDF: 978-1-5013-2457-4
ePub: 978-1-5013-2456-7

Series: The Study of Sound

Cover design and cover image by Liron Gilenberg

Typeset by Deanta Publishing Services, Chennai, India

To find out more about our authors and books visit www.bloomsbury.com. Here you will find extracts, author interviews, details of forthcoming events, and the option to sign up for our newsletters.

CONTENTS

Introduction 1

1 The Sound of Nonsense 7

2 The Sound of the Page 23

3 Silly Noises 45

4 Pop Hearts Nonsense 67

Conclusion 99

Notes 105
Bibliography 129
Discography 135
Videography 139
Index 140

Introduction

'Watch the sense and the sounds will take care of themselves', so says the Duchess in *Alice's Adventures in Wonderland*.[1] But can we be so sure of this? The Duchess, like her creator Lewis Carroll, seems to put more emphasis on the sound of words than their sense. This aspect of her character has been much remarked upon, not least by those interested in the role that sound plays in creating meaning and nonsense.[2] As some of Carroll's readers would have known, he himself was playing with sound when he placed these words in the Duchess's mouth; her 'moral' is based on the English proverb 'take care of the pence and the pounds will take care of themselves'. It is only one of many instances in Carroll's work where the work of nonsense – what Marnie Parsons has called 'nonsense strategies' – relies on sound to do its business.[3] This book responds to that reliance by highlighting the importance of sound in understanding the nonsense of writers such as Carroll and Edward Lear, as well as James Joyce, before connecting this noisy writing to works which engage more directly with sound, including sound poetry, experimental music and pop. By emphasizing sonic factors, I try to amplify the connections between a wide range of artistic examples and to build a case for the importance of sound in creating, maintaining and disrupting meaning.

Nonsense literature, particularly that associated with the English tradition made famous by Carroll and Lear, has generated a rich and varied body of study in a variety of disciplines, including literature, linguistics, art history, philosophy and psychology. Much of this exegesis has focused on questions of meaning and the 'logic of sense' or on questions of normality and abnormality. Invariably focused on words and sentences as they appear on the page, few studies of nonsense take sound as their primary analytical perspective. I take this gap as my starting point and, while engaging with many of the other things that have been said about my chosen examples, I hinge my study on the sonic dimensions of nonsense.

The first chapter offers an overview of some of the ways in which nonsense has been approached, noting the difficulties in defining terms and agreeing on boundaries. By way of my own definitions, I suggest types of nonsense that bind the diverse examples to be found through the rest of the book. I also start to offer observations on the role of sound in creating, maintaining and disrupting sense. The second chapter is focused on the resonance of the page and, in addition to nonsense literature, includes discussion of modernist literature. More work has been done in recent years on the role of sound in modernist writing – particularly James Joyce – and my aim here is to highlight sounds which are pertinent to a discussion of nonsense and to set up connections with music, for example by considering how the work of writers such as Carroll and Joyce has been auralized or musicalized. Having established the importance of sound on the written page, the book moves to work that more directly challenged the written dimension of literature by engaging with sound as a primary text; examples include artists and theorists associated with a variety of European art 'movements' (futurism, Dada, surrealism), sound poets such as Hugo Ball, Henri Chopin and Bob Cobbing, and the audio–visual cut-up experiments of Brion Gysin and William Burroughs. Here I'm interested in sonic challenges, be they chopped audio or sonic palimpsests, and the efforts required to get at meaning.

One of the aims of the book is to show connections between modernist, avant-garde or experimental artists and those more associated with popular culture, so, in keeping with a starting point of Carroll and Lear, the project also investigates the importance of nonsense sounds in popular music. Chapter 4 – the longest – is devoted to popular music and the importance of nonsense in popular song, taking in scat singing, vocalese, doo-wop, early rock 'n' roll, yodelling, hip-hop, singer-songwriters and artists who have created their own languages in which to sing. The relationships between words, sense and music are important here. One suggestion is that the shift from words to music is – from a linguistic perspective – often accompanied by a shift to nonsense, but that this linguistic nonsense becomes subject to another kind of musicalized sense-making. The process can also be witnessed in reverse; vocal sounds used to emulate musical instruments (e.g. in scat, doo-wop or other mouth music) can be heard as proto-words and the point at which they are heard as such is what I call the *nonsense moment*. Nonsense functions in these instances as the overlapping territory between non-semantic vocables and clearly understood, meaningful words.

In tracing this trajectory, I am interested in how written, spoken and sung linguistic elements – predominantly words, parts of words and elements of phrases – create nonsense moments that rely on sound in one form or another. To make the kind of connections I am making between written and sonic texts requires an acceptance of the interrelationships between what Don Ihde calls 'the word as soundful' and 'sounds as meaningful':

> The philosopher, concerned with comprehensiveness, must eventually call for attention to the *word as soundful*. On the other side, the sciences that attend to the soundful, from phonetics to acoustics, do so as if the sound were bare and empty of significance in a physics of the soundful. And the philosopher, concerned with the roots of reflection in human experience, must eventually also listen to the *sounds as meaningful*.[4]

Like Ihde, I am interested in sound as it is experienced phenomenologically, although I mix this approach with awareness of intertextuality and intermediality. For me, the knowledge of a text's precursors – and this includes one's lack of, or partial, knowledge of them – is part of the phenomena available to the perceiving subject. This awareness, which I see as a grasping after meaning by a sometimes bewildered subject, is also what makes up the nonsense moment. This is the moment in perception when one is beyond, between or ahead of the moment of ascertaining sense. It is a glitch moment, a temporary period of blurring, the point in the process of code-switching where the codes are muddled.

Hopefully, the examples provided throughout the book will help clarify what I mean by this. I flag it up here, however, to anticipate some potential issues that readers may have regarding my definitions of nonsense, the ambitious scope of this short book and the connections I am making between my various examples. I approach the issue of definitions and typologies of nonsense more fully in the next chapter. For now, it's important to note that this is a book about nonsense, not solely about nonsense literature, though nonsense literature is a recurring presence. When it comes to nonsense and music, some may well take exception to scat, doo-wop or vocalese being referred to as nonsense because these vocal techniques have been categorized for musicology as musical, not verbal practices. My response here is to challenge such absolutist definitions of these musical processes and to ask instead why so many other people before me have made similar connections to mine. Were such listeners 'wrong' to do so? There is no hard and fast boundary between nonsense syllables used for musical effect and those same syllables used as words in a lyric. When Gene Vincent sings 'Be-bop-a-lula, she's my baby', or when the Edsels sing 'I got a girl named Rama Lama, Rama Lama Ding Dong', how can we know if they are imitating instruments or referring to nicknames? The syntax of such utterances hangs in the balance.

Having given several spoken presentations on this project, I have been heartened by not only my audiences' willingness to recognize many of the connections I am trying to make, but also the enthusiasm with which further examples have been offered. Given that I have had to severely edit the mass of examples I had already collected, it has been difficult to make space for many of these additions, but their existence reassures me that the concepts with which I'm dealing have resonance for others. If my selection of nonsense writers, sound poets and pop musicians is necessarily restricted to particular eras and genres, I trust that the points I am making can be applied by readers to other examples. I hope too that, just because there are many other examples from the history of literature and music that could be defined as nonsense according to my usage, my omission of them does not weaken my arguments.

When considering the scope of my project and the wide net I am casting, I have attempted to stay true to the objectives of the series in which it appears. One of these is to use a single concept to illustrate the interdisciplinary nature of sound studies. In my case, that single concept is nonsense, but the perspectives and examples through which I approach the concept are designed to encourage interdisciplinarity. Another way of putting this is to say that I have attempted to make the book short but provocative, not seeking to answer all the questions it poses nor to lock down discussion of any of the areas it touches on. This is not a licence to vagueness or lack of rigour, but rather a recognition that this book series sets out to offer something different to longer, specialist monographs.

I have wanted to respond to the vitality of nonsense and to revel in connections. Again, this may suggest a potential lack of historical or other contextual specificity to the examples cited. It may be felt, for example, that I enjoy listening for similarities at the expense of adequately exploring differences. I must admit to an enjoyment of staging my own Mad Hatters party, perhaps sitting Edward Lear next to Little Richard, Hugo Ball next to David Byrne, and Lewis Carroll next to Bob Cobbing and Ivor Cutler. But while I wish to at least imply a levelling process regarding the cultural provenance of my examples, I am never suggesting outright equivalency. As with many comparative methods, it is more about asking what light can be cast – what sound can be projected – by placing together the products of seemingly disparate cultural worlds. The artist Christian Marclay, responding to a question about the equivalence of objects placed together in some of his projects even when those objects have little relation to each other, makes the following observation:

> But the reason they are together is to offer a third reading, totally disconnected from their initial usage. They tell a beautiful story together. Like if you're writing poetry, you put together two words that rhyme or off-rhyme, and even though they may be unrelated, that rhyme is going to give the phrase a different weight. It kind of forces them together.[5]

Similar notions have been expressed through some of the other artistic processes I discuss in this book, such as the cut-ups of Brion Gysin and William Burroughs, the plunderphonics of John Oswald, and the 'rhyming' of doo-wop, country music and sound poetry undertaken by Paul Dutton. The idea is there, too, in the practices carried out by a whole host of DJs and other composers whose mixings, matchings and mismatchings provide the ideal soundtrack to mad tea parties.

1

The Sound of Nonsense

Nonsense Definitions

Before proceeding further, it would be as well to explain what I mean by 'nonsense' and to do so with reference to other writers' attempts at definition. The first thing to establish is that most writing in English on nonsense is about, or at least has its starting point in, the tradition of *nonsense literature*, which is also the starting point for my study. However, one of the problems that emerges from the eliding of nonsense and nonsense literature is the tendency to make sweeping statements about the former which are only really relevant to nonsense literature quite narrowly defined. Wim Tigges's 1988 study, for example, is presented as *An Anatomy of Literary Nonsense*, yet drops the 'literary' specification for a section entitled 'What Nonsense is Not'.[1] While my starting point in the next chapter is literary nonsense, my study subsequently covers other disciplines and therefore requires a broader definition of nonsense, towards which this chapter will work. For now, it should be noted that many of the attempts at definition below emanate from the long history of critical commentary on nonsense literature.[2]

In *The Field of Nonsense*, her classic commentary from 1952, Elizabeth Sewell writes, 'The assumption that you know what sense is, and consequently what nonsense is, depends not on the acceptance or rejection of blocs of fact but upon the adoption of certain sets of mental relations. Whatever holds together according to these relationships will be sense, whatever does not will be nonsense.'[3] For Sewell, context is everything and meaning is contingent upon it. There is no absolute nonsense any more than there is absolute sense; subjects establish and develop sense-making processes for themselves and those processes reflect and resound back on the subject. Jean-Jacques Lecercle, one of the best writers on nonsense, suggests that 'the negative prefix in "nonsense" ... is the mark of a process not merely of denial but also of reflexivity' and that 'non-sense is also meta-sense'.[4] This helps to define nonsense as a deliberate strategy – for example, one used by nonsense writers, comedians, sound artists and musicians – and this is an idea I will return to. This usage also contrasts with the use of 'nonsense' as a dismissive description ('stuff and nonsense!'), where it is the reader–critic who decides rather than the original author.

Nonsense writer Mervyn Peake, reflecting on Lewis Carroll's work, spoke of the 'madness' of nonsense, a madness of the imagination and therefore more 'lovely' than that associated with pathology:

> Nonsense can be gentle or riotous. It can clank like a stone in the empty bucket of fatuity. It can take you by the hand and lead you nowhere. ... It swims, plunges, cavorts, and rises in its own element. It's a fabulous fowl. For *non-sense* is not the opposite of good sense. That would be 'Bad Sense'. It's something quite apart – and isn't the opposite of anything.[5]

Robert Maslen, editor of Peake's *Complete Nonsense*, follows this up by suggesting nonsense as 'an arrangement of words on the page without regard to meaning but with careful regard to grammar, form, sound and rhythm'.[6] This definition again falls on the side of the producer of nonsense, and on nonsense as a strategy; usefully for my own study, it also highlights the role of sound in the workings of the nonsense text. Like Peake, Michael Heyman emphasizes the importance of play and process in his description of nonsense: 'a particular *kind* of play, one that is not pure exuberance, not unrestrained joy and, above all, not gibberish (though all of these are often elements of it). Rather, it is an art form rooted in sophisticated aesthetics, linguistics and play with logic, and it is the *art* of nonsense that is one of its most appealing aspects.'[7]

Noel Malcolm, in the introduction to *The Origins of English Nonsense*, justifies his decision not to precisely define nonsense by arguing that 'definition-making is not necessary for practical reasons, any more than it is necessary for studies of lyric poetry or comedy to begin with watertight definitions of those terms'. Nor is it desirable, he continues, 'for theoretical reasons either, since these literary types are cluster-concepts: they have a core on which all can agree, and a more variable periphery on which disagreement is always possible.'[8] Yet, Malcolm does appear to be at greater ease with what we might call anti-definitions and peppers his study with examples that are clearly marked as 'not nonsense'. Of these, the following is useful in that it gets at a relationship – at times a tension – evident in this book, that between the literary and the sonic:

> Nonsense language is, of course, a type of nonsense; it presents the form of meaning while denying us the substance. But the denial is so complete that it can go no further; it is unable to perform that exploration of nonsense possibilities in which proper nonsense literature excels. Apart from creating a generic nonsense effect, gibberish is capable of performing only one trick, which is to make funny noises. To achieve any other effects, it must dilute itself with words (or at least recognisable vestiges of words) which are not nonsense.[9]

For now, what I wish to take from this anti-definition of nonsense is, first, the subdivision of nonsense into other components such as 'nonsense language' and 'gibberish' and, secondly, the idea, repeated by numerous commentators, that nonsense requires a certain amount of regulation, logic and coherence to succeed as nonsense. This accords with the view taken by Jacqueline Flescher, who writes, 'The backbone of nonsense must be a consciously regulated pattern. It can be the rhythmic structure of verse, the order of legal procedure, or the rules of the chess-game. Implicitly or explicitly, these three variations are all present in *Alice*.'[10]

For my own purposes, I am particularly interested in the 'funny noises' that Malcolm alludes to and, now that *gibberish* has been invoked, we might pause to recall other synonyms of, or words related to, nonsense: *gobbledygook, drivel, twaddle, mumbo-jumbo, tosh, balderdash, babble, chatter, bunkum, hogwash, jargon*. Some of these words can be associated with the subset of nonsense that Malcolm refers to as 'nonsense language', while others are more clearly related to forms of criticism. When Max Eastman refers to Gertrude Stein's *Tender Buttons* as 'mumbo-jumbo', for example, we know that we are supposed to take it as harsh criticism; so too when Adam Piette, in his *Remembering and the Sound of Words*, dismisses Julia Kristeva's theories as 'the ruinous rhyme between childish babble and psychobabble'.[11] This use of nonsense-related words as criticism is interesting in that it invariably uncovers a resentment on the part of the user of the word which contrasts strongly with the playful usage of nonsense in the classic literature of Carroll, Lear and other authors of nonsense literature. While seemingly quite distinct, these uses of nonsense (as accusation or strategy) can often be found coexisting, as when Alice dismisses what the Queen of Hearts says as 'Stuff and nonsense!'[12] As for gibberish, the world it summons is described by Stephen Fry as 'a strangely familiar land, yet one in which nothing is linguistically as it seems', which might well pass as a description of nonsense too. However, while 'one man's gibberish may be another woman's native tongue', Fry maintains a distinction between gibberish and nonsense, with the latter having a greater reliance on logic and therefore more coherent meaning.[13]

Then there's *logorrhoea*, the 'tendency to extreme loquacity' (OED), an excessive wordiness often associated with extreme psychological conditions. Jean-Jacques Lecercle mentions logorrhoea as an example of nonsense where 'too much signifies, and too little is signified' and where 'the abundance of words balances the lack of meaning'.[14] Lecercle uses his own term, *délire*, to refer to 'an utterance which, at the very moment when it plays havoc with language acknowledges the domination of the rules it transgresses'.[15] These types of nonsense are not generally those of the classic tradition of Carroll and Lear but can be found in writers of earlier generations (François Rabelais, Laurence Sterne) and later ones (James Joyce, Gertrude Stein, William Burroughs, Julián Ríos). Lecercle frequently makes comparisons between writers of nonsense literature and later modernists, arguing that, for the latter, *délire* is wielded as a destructive agent. Writing about Antonin Artaud, Lecercle states, 'Nonsense as a genre always strives towards the linguistic security of the mimetic; hence the strictures of Artaud, whose poetic stance is that of modernism: a position of negation and rejection. The modernist text asserts itself by rejecting mimesis – often pejoratively labelled "realism".'[16]

For understandable reasons – mainly a desire to clearly delineate a field of study – some writers on nonsense have wanted to make distinctions between nonsense literature proper (as they see it) and other forms of nonsense, such as those listed above. As we have already heard, Noel Malcolm makes a distinction between nonsense literature, gibberish and the 'noise' of nonsense language more generally. It is important for Malcolm to make this distinction not only because he wishes to defend nonsense literature as a cherished and particular art form, but also because he wishes to challenge what he sees as the generally agreed-upon origins of the form in the nineteenth century by asserting its creation in the seventeenth. I would argue that it is because of the corralling of nonsense into nonsense literature that the role of sound has been neglected in favour of the textual and that it is time to attend more dutifully to those 'funny noises' which are so crucial to most nonsense, literary or otherwise. What's more, the division of nonsense into extremes of absolute gibberish and nonsense literature is a false one, with most nonsense art occupying some position in that 'diluted' in-between area. There are no obvious boundaries, and it is precisely the blurry play of boundary-crossing in which nonsense revels. For such reasons, I find Lecercle's gradated instances of *délire* more convincing than Malcolm's outright categorizations. As for the business of origins, I pitch myself closer to those who have looked at longer and broader histories of nonsense, those that reach not only for historical precursors and successors of the nonsense literature tradition, but also for related practices arising in other art forms associated with the word and the voice, including sound poetry, experimental art, comedy and music. In doing so, I feel a certain sense of shared mission to recent studies of nonsense that have appeared in print and broadcast media.[17]

There is a sense of exhaustion in defining nonsense. As Michael Heyman has observed, 'there are as many definitions of sense, nonsense, and literary nonsense as there are critics'.[18] Several writers, Malcolm among them, have suggested that nonsense is something we may not be able to define precisely but which we recognize when we see it. Yet such seemingly open and flexible approaches to defining nonsense are often belied by references to 'real' or 'proper' nonsense or claims that such and such an example is 'not really nonsense'. Given my focus on sound in this book, I proceed at times with an understanding that nonsense is something we know when we hear it and I have restricted my use of negative definitions of the 'this is not real nonsense' type. No doubt some readers will find fault with what I include as nonsense but this seems to be a risk that no nonsensologist can escape. If, like other writers on nonsense, I am unable to provide a neat definition, I will posit as a starting point five types of nonsense that I have in mind for what follows:

1 That which introduces altered logic even when 'normal' language is used. This would be the realm of Carroll and his followers or of Goonesque comedy.
2 That which stays within a 'normal' syntactic regime but introduces glitches and other disruptive strategies and plays with the logic of semantics. Modernist and postmodernist writers and musicians would be among the examples of this type.
3 That which emerges from altering syntax to create magic, confusion or truth. This would include cut-ups, permutations and other strategies that play with the logics of syntax.
4 That which borders on or overlaps with the absurd. This would include Beckettian drama and Dylanesque songwriting.
5 That which uses codes or terms only understood by specialists or insiders. This is only 'nonsense' for non-specialists or outsiders, what we might more commonly think of as gobbledygook or jargon. This includes hip language like jazz jive, hip-hop slang, subcultural terms, certain academic discourse and the BBC Shipping Forecast.

Connecting these is the nonsense moment, that space of bewilderment between two or more modes of meaning where sense-making is forced into code-switching. Ultimately, there are many types and many definitions. For this book, I want to keep what nonsense means broad and to express my interest in the connections between these various ways in which sense is put up against its other(s). My list of nonsense types is a guide and not a set of rules.

Sound and Sense

If, as Susan Stewart has suggested, the fascination with nonsense resides in its being 'language lifted out of context, language turning on itself, language as infinite regression, language made hermetic, opaque in an envelope of language', then it is necessary to consider the importance of sound in all these processes and in sense-making more generally.[19] It is striking how well Stewart's description would work as a description of sound poetry, of what might be called 'vocable art' (non-semantic singing, vocalese, scatting, some forms of rapping) or of the manipulation of sonic communication by mechanical means (tape loops, sampling, mixing and remixing). It is also notable how Stewart's use of 'envelope' echoes and anticipates work on what has been called 'the sonorous envelope'. One of the more focused applications of such ideas to music is David Schwartz's *Listening Subjects*, in which the author analyses a range of twentieth-century musical examples from a psychoanalytic perspective. Schwartz explores the notion of the sonorous envelope in an analysis of the early tape loops of Steve Reich, noting how the obsessive repetition and breaking down of everyday language lead to an estrangement of sense. Mechanical manipulation allows for a kind of reversal of the process by which infants learn to make sense of the world, first as fragmented, non-meaning and later as increasingly meaningful sound elements that can be combined in order to communicate with others.[20] While I have not followed a psychoanalytic approach in this book, the notion of the sonorous envelope does correspond, to an extent, with what I am calling the nonsense moment, that blurry space between worlds of meaning where we find ourselves grasping after sense.

Other estranging devices can be found in religious practices, such as the chanting of mantras or repetition of holy names, phrases and prayers. On a more secular level, children's games, jokes, slips of the tongue and other 'perversions' of language, as well as the learning of new languages or songs, all orientate us towards the otherwise 'inaudible' role of sound itself in our everyday communication. It is surprising, then, that much of the abundant literature on nonsense has been relatively silent on the role of sound in readers' ability to make sense of nonsense writers. There are exceptions to this tendency. Stewart, for example, attends to the sonic dimensions of nonsense at frequent points in her study, no doubt partly due to her focus on folklore and popular practices. Indeed, two of the most useful conclusions which can be drawn from Stewart's work are that the study of nonsense literature forces a consideration of the literature as indebted to popular practice and that literature's populism is often best expressed by its reliance on, and experimentation with, sound. In the 1940s, T. S. Eliot described nonsense poetry's proximity to music and James Rother, identifying the nonsense style in Eliot and other modernist writers, notes these writers' reliance on twentieth-century sound in a way that foregrounds contemporary music technology:

> In one way or another it has been necessary for all serious poets in this century to come to terms with [modern vernacular culture], whether it be in the bitter and facetious manner chosen by E. E. Cummings [sic] or in the visionary exuberance of a poem like [Hart Crane's] *The Bridge*. Eliot's technique for turning each of these 'media' to his own poetic advantage was quite simply one of 'moog' eclecticism, of soundmixing whereby the inflectional idiosyncrasies of personal speech (edited almost as though they were separate tapes) could be 'synthesized' into a generalized dialect of Anglo-American civilization.[21]

For all of this, these writers are mainly known for their written works. A more radical interrogation of sound and sense can be found in the development of sound poetry, the contemporary history of which corresponds neatly with the history of phonographic sound, as if the experience of the recorded voice was necessary for the realization of what could be done with the voice in live performance. This is an area I will return to in Chapter 3.

One way to look at this sense-making is to consider what happens when, in the midst of an unfolding sentence, we come across words with which we are unfamiliar. The unfamiliarity may be due to various factors, including the difficulty, technicality or foreignness of the word in question; equally, as is the case in much nonsense literature, the word may be placed precisely to confuse, amuse or intrigue us. Michael Heyman notes this process in the work of Edward Lear, citing the use of the word 'mucilaginous' in the following passage from Lear's *Story of Four Little Children Who Went Round the World*: 'The Blue-Bottle-Flies began to buzz at once in a sumptuous and sonorous manner, the melodious and mucilaginous sounds echoing all over the waters, and resounding across the tumultuous tops of the transitory Titmice upon the intervening and verdant mountains.' Heyman states:

The definition of 'mucilaginous' does not fit this context, nor does it resemble an appropriate word; the word represents a semantic blank, yet the mind tries to bridge this gap by forming some image, an image which is negated soon after its inception. By a stretch of the imagination, we can try to imagine a beautiful, echoing sound to be 'mucilaginous,' but whatever we imagine remains arbitrary, however resonant and evocative the word may be. We try to create the impossible sense-context behind a word which neither has nor can have one. We must also remember that the adult and the child will react differently to this device of nonsense – that the child does not know the real meaning of the word and therefore has a different problem from the adult, who knows the meaning and must deal with the obvious incongruity.[22]

Perhaps 'mucilaginous' is an appropriate word for sound after all, referring as it does to a sticky or gummy quality such as that produced by certain plants (and, contra Heyman, how many adults really know this?). Perhaps sound can be sticky – it can certainly seem sludgy, for example in a poorly mastered recording. Sludginess and stickiness also seem appropriate to the murky depths of the mind. Regardless, it is clear that adult and child have a different awareness of what they know and what they don't, yet both find themselves in a nonsense moment, grasping after sense.

Another way to think about the unfolding or blocking of sonic sense is to consider challenges posed in the process of hearing *anything*. Douglas Kahn considers the situation from the perspective of the listener with hearing difficulties:

> Partial deafness and noise breed and feed on homophony, a device that almost always operates unconsciously as a salvaging maneuver but that can also be used more deliberately as a source of enjoyment. While resourcefully weaving phonemes and vocables through anticipation and recursion, generating options and making choices of what may be appropriate or at least plausible in the context, the range of communications can be an arena for play and for entertaining difference toward whatever ends.[23]

Kahn connects this salvaging procedure to the example of encountering a foreign language, where 'the urge against all odds to continuously make meaning from linguistic noise is very strong'.[24] This process correlates with that posited by Jean-Luc Nancy as a difference between hearing and listening: 'If "to hear" is to understand the sense ... to listen is to be straining toward a possible meaning, and consequently one that is not immediately accessible.' This leads Nancy to a further distinction, that between listening to 'a speech we want to understand' and listening to a piece of music; in the former, 'listening strains towards a present sense beyond sound', while in the latter 'it is from sound itself that sense is offered to auscultation'. Yet, realizing a distinction may fix itself between sound and sense, Nancy quickly asserts that the main distinction to be drawn is that between hearing and listening, for in the latter – whether focused on speech or music – 'sound and sense mix together and resonate in each other, or through each other'.[25] I find this damping of the sound/sense and music/speech distinctions welcome for the musical examples I will be covering later, most of which place a strong emphasis on musicalized words (a complication Nancy does not need to consider given that he seems mainly to be considering instrumental music). While I'm aware that not all listeners may place the emphasis I do on the meaning of words in songs, it is precisely the presence of words, in my hearing, that leads to nonsense moments. Listeners confronted with semi-coherent babble may create alternate words to those which were emitted. Listeners too, no less than readers, utilize what Marnie Parsons calls 'a syntactical impulse' in using syntax as a way for dealing with semantic lapses.[26] This can lead to the well-known issue of misheard lyrics, where auditors become convinced of the words they have substituted for those actually sung, sometimes even maintaining this conviction long after discovering their error.

Michael Heyman, introducing a collection of Indian nonsense, claims a near universality for 'the sheer joy in the musicality of language, its sound and rhythm. Nonsense writers are often more concerned with the sound than the sense and pull out all the tools of euphony.' Yet, no doubt recognizing the danger of splitting sound from sense too decisively, Heyman continues, 'a nonsense world emerges because of the *nature* and *sound* of the language used, rather than language simply being used to describe a world'. Nonsense language may signify 'more by resonance than reference' but its connection of sense-making ensures it functions 'in more ways than just as word-music'.[27]

The Russian poet Velimir Khlebnikov, famed for the co-creation (with Alexei Kruchenykh) of *zaum* poetry, similarly attended to the ways in which sound and sense work together. In an essay on contemporary poetry published in 1920, Khlebnikov wrote, 'The word leads a double life. Sometimes ... the sound element lives in a self-sufficient life, while the particle of sense named by the word stands in shadow. At other times the word is subservient to sense, and then sense ceases to be "all-powerful" and autocratic.' Although Khlebnikov appears to offer a similar distinction between sense and sound as that found in other writers ('Either a land radiant with meaning or a land radiant with sound', he writes), he also suggests a more dialectical relationship: 'This struggle between two worlds, between two powers, goes on eternally in every word and gives a double life to language: two possible orbits for two spinning stars. In one form of creativity, sense turns in a circular path about sound; in the other sound turns about sense.'[28] Moreover, it is worth noting that he is here analysing the work of his contemporaries; his own experimental poetry differs considerably from those he is writing about by queering the orbits to bring sound and sense into a collision course. As his translator Paul Schmidt observes, 'Khlebnikov's writing displays a perpetual willingness to allow form to form itself. He allows accidents to happen. A primary note in Khlebnikov's writing as I read it is the sense of wonder at the play of language, of sound allowed to move freely in search of its own sense.'[29]

Imitation and Foreign Languages

When thinking about the relationship between sound and sense, it can be useful to consider imitation as a way of understanding the world. This may take the form of the mimetic facilities we use as infants, the (often unconscious) use of onomatopoeia in everyday conversation, singing along to a piece of music, trying on another person's voice or accent, attempting to emulate non-human sounds, learning a foreign language, and so on. A recurring feature of music cultures is the desire to emulate the phenomena of the world by using voices and instruments to echo and expand sonic experience. Animals and birds are a common thread and our versions of their sounds provide music to our ears even as they make nonsense of song lyrics. The cuckoos of 'Sumer Is Icumen In' have resounded in England from at least the thirteenth century. Tomás Méndez's 'Cucurrucucú Paloma', a twentieth-century musical cousin, has travelled from Mexico throughout the world. J. P. Das's 'Vain Cock' ('Poda Kapala' in Oriya) was useless; instead of speaking its owner's language ('ku-ku-du-koo'), it would only say 'cock-a-doodle-doo' (it soon showed up on the barbeque).[30] Then there's Ivor Cutler's 'Cockadoodledon't', in which a little yellow shoe is thrown at a bird, a pink tomato sandwich, Santa Claus, an elephant, a granny and a cobbler, all of whom start singing 'cockadoodledon't' in response.[31] The nonsense tradition is replete with humans mimicking animals and vice versa. The interimitation of humans and animals (albeit exclusively the product of human imagination) corresponds to the 'interorientation' that Bakhtin detects in the carnivalesque obsession with topsy-turvydom and the bodily grotesque.[32]

If birds and beasts offer one kind of imitable music, people who speak other languages provide another. As Don Ihde writes, 'The foreign tongue is first a kind of music before it becomes a language; it is first pregnant with meaning before the meaning is delivered to me.' For Elizabeth Sewell, 'One's own mother-tongue is sense, the remainder are so much Greek or double dutch', while Marnie Parsons suggests, 'Language is at its most musical (or is appreciated with a most musical frame of mind) when it is not comprehensible, when its phonotextual aspects are short-circuited.'[33] One of the ways this musicality is approached is through imitation, as in the 1973 song 'Prisencolinensinainciusol' by Italian comedian Adriano Celentano.[34] Celentano wrote the song to express how popular American song sounded to him as a non-native speaker of English. As David Bellos notes, 'the transcription of "anglo-gibberish" in textual form represents English-soundingness only when it is vocalized (aloud, or in your head) according to the standard rules for vocalizing *Italian* script. *Prisencolinensinainciusol* ... is a specifically Italian fiction of the foreign.'[35] Bellos also refers to the 'Mother Goose' rhymes published by Luis van Rooten in 1967, in which the famous nursery rhyme 'Humpty Dumpty sat on a wall' is 'translated' into French as 'Un petit d'un petit s'étonne aux Halles', which is a homophonic translation rather than a semantic one (reading the translated text with a French accent gives the best effect). The French words are real enough but don't mean a great deal and have only the sonic relationship with the original.[36]

If translation can be a kind of nonsense – and Bellos and Umberto Eco have provided many examples to show that it can[37] – the issue of translating something that is already nonsense in its first language is a trickier matter altogether. Michael Heyman has collected many examples of Indian nonsense and has been faced with the challenge of translating them to English. He cites Alice and the Red Queen's discussion of whether 'fiddle-de-dee' can be translated to French and notes the importance of sound in translation: 'Because the sound of nonsense is often at least as important as the sense, we have made extra effort to retain the play and music of the original languages.'[38] Going back further, can mock Latin mixed with sixteenth-century French be translated into English? The translators of Rabelais show that it can. In Chapter 19 of *Gargantua*, Master Janotus de Bragmardo pleads with Gargantua to return the bells he has stolen from Notre Dame, arguing that the sound of the bells is necessary for the health of the wine grapes: winemakers 'wanted to buy them for the quasimodal quality of the elementary complexion that is enthronified in the terresterility of their quidditative nature to extraneise the fogs and fierce storms on our vineyards'. Janotus's speech is used by Rabelais to satirize the logorrheic qualities of formal and pseudoformal address. Ramping up the absurdity, he has Janotus inject numerous examples of Latin gibberish into his speech, reaching a peak of sonic nonsense which Andrew Brown translates as: 'Look I'll prove that you should give [the bells] back to me. Ergo sic argumentor: omnis dingalinga dingalingabilis in dingalingerio dingilingando dingalingans, dingalingativo dingalingare facit dingalingabiliter dingalingantes.'[39] Brown has presumably chosen 'ding' as the basis for the mutated Latin due to its onomatopoeic resonance, one found in many songs (the Christmas carol 'Ding Dong Merrily on High', for example, or the Ronettes' 'Sleigh Ride' with its 'ring-a-ling-a-ling-a-ding-dong-ding').

The Social Life of Nonsense

As we have seen, scholars of nonsense have been drawn to hear unknown languages as musical, whether as sites where sound overcomes sense or where non-comprehension alerts listeners to the sonicity of the unknown. It's also worth considering how we try to make sense in sound, to grasp after meaning, or at least a sense of a meaning. While we might be tempted to attempt it when listening to birdsong or the bark of a pet dog, it is more likely that we will try to do so when human mouths are making noises that sound something like words. As Stephen Rudy writes, in an introduction to the linguistic theories of Roman Jakobson, 'any sound sequence within language, even if in a foreign or unknown tongue, is categorically different from natural sounds or music, and thus demands a meaning, even if purely differential or relational'.[40] It is this sense of the relational that has led me to an interest in what I call the social life of nonsense, a term which could describe any communal sharing of, or enjoyment in, nonsensical utterances, but which I'm thinking about more specifically in terms of the internet and social media. While researching the many varied examples of nonsense that I have considered for this book, I have been struck by the connections the online community makes between different cultural texts. At times, these have coincided with connections I have also made; at other times, they have led me to trails on which I found examples new to me or connections I had never considered. I found that the relational meaning to which Rudy refers was crucial to the way in which connections are made online. If we consider nonsense phenomenologically, as part of the way we sense – and make sense of – the world that presents itself to us, then these relational aspects become important. What I call the nonsense moment is a borderline experience, sited between other realms of sense-making; the very nature of 'understanding' or not is part of the nonsense process.

Consider, for example, the comments accompanying a YouTube clip of Dutch composer/performer Jaap Blonk performing Kurt Schwitters's sound poem *Ursonate*, a work completed in the early 1930s. Many refer, understandably, to more recent works of popular culture: one person writes 'Would be right at home on sesame street'; another comments 'Ratatatay brought me here', referring to a song by Chumbawamba about singer George Melly's use of the *Ursonate* to scare off muggers; a third writes, 'Ski-Bi dibby dib yo da dub dub Yo dab dub dub Ski-Bi dibby dib yo da dub dub Yo dab dub dub I'm the Scatman', referring to the 1994 hit by John Paul Larkin (Scatman John).[41] Such responses can be seen as relational sense-making activities and/or nonsense strategies that deliberately combine disparate elements via a perceived sonic relationship. A browser with enough time and curiosity might follow some of those connections, which in turn will lead to more, while the algorithms of the side bar make further suggestions. In my case, following the lead to Scatman John's video, I was then taken to WatchMojo's list of '10 Most Hated Songs', which included plenty of musical nonsense (or gibberish), including Hampton the Hampster's 'Hampster Dance', Crazy Frog's remix of 'Axel F' and Las Ketchup's 'The Ketchup Song (Aserejé)'.[42] From there it was a short slide through YouTube's looking-glass to the world of nonsense-based memes.

Returning to Jaap Blonk's performance of the *Ursonate*, there were also several expressions of baffled dismissal accompanying the video clip. For further evidence of the failure of different texts to move beyond their contexts, it is worth reading Blonk's account of his unpopular performances of the *Ursonate* at punk gigs in the 1980s, in particular his experience as the opening act for the Stranglers at a 1986 gig in Utrecht in front of 2000 concertgoers. But perhaps it is wrong to class such cognitive disruptions as failures; instead we should consider that the *Ursonate* was continuing its work of upsetting the status quo. In the case of Blonk's Utrecht concert, what the response really underlined was the sonic conservatism of Stranglers fans in the mid-1980s. As Blonk writes, 'The next morning one newspaper had the headline "Jaap Blonk Shocks Punk Audience With Dada Poetry," which for me was a nice testimony to the fact that Schwitters' piece was still very much alive, in spite of its age.'[43] Some of the YouTube commenters make the same point, noting that the poem is still doing its work if it is getting angry or dismissive responses.

We will return to the 'silly noises' of sound poetry in Chapter 3. In this chapter, I have set out the framework within which I am considering the sound of nonsense. In the rest of the book, I revisit the idea of the nonsense moment and the relationship between words, sounds and sense. My nonsense typology, meanwhile, informs the many examples which follow.

2

The Sound of the Page

In recent years, a growing number of scholars are being drawn towards the ways in which, to use Marnie Parson's evocative description, 'elements of sound stalk through printed language raising the reader's spirits'.[1] As sound studies and literary studies come together, the noises that go into books have started to be listened to with renewed interest. This has always been an interest to those who study poetry and, given the poetic nature of much nonsense literature, it is perhaps unsurprising that phonology plays a role in nonsense scholarship, even if it is rarely a primary role. Jean-Jacques Lecercle attests to the importance of sound in Lewis Carroll's work when he observes that the nonsense words used in the poem 'Jabberwocky' defy visualization despite the best efforts of Humpty Dumpty and John Tenniel:

> We do not spontaneously read the poem with an eye to Tenniel's drawings, or like the authors of those linguistic textbooks: *the words sing in our ears*, unexpected links are established between them, relationships of alliteration, assonance or rhyme, of potential spoonerism ... of leisurely exploration of phonetic similarities.[2]

Similarly, in the introduction to Mervyn Peake's *Complete Nonsense*, Robert Maslen writes that 'words chosen for their sound and rhythm ... acquire a vigorous life of their own, determining the direction of a narrative in verse or prose'.[3] In this chapter, I consider examples from nonsense and modernist literature, firstly as written texts which rely on sound, then as texts which have been auralized through recorded readings and musical adaptation.

Nonsense literature

Lecercle sees nonsense literature as 'a conservative-revolutionary genre': conservative in that it respects rules, regulations, propriety and authority; revolutionary in that it plays havoc with norms and introduces subversion and rebellion into the domestic text.[4] While the havoc that Lecercle identifies with nonsense is the delirious play with logic, sense and inter-character relations, we can detect it also in the recurring noisiness and uncouthness of the classic texts. Nonsense literature is a noisy genre, whether in the constant gabbling of the characters in the Alice books or the often violent and cacophonous situations described by Lear. As an example of the latter, consider the extreme 'hullaballoo' described in the 1872 poem 'The Scroobious Pip'. When the Scroobious Pip goes out into the world, it attracts the attention of 'all the beasts in the world', resulting in a serious racket. With the howling of the Wolf, the neighing of the Horse, the squeaking of the Pig, the braying of the Donkey and the roaring of the Lion, 'there never was heard such a noise before'. The clamour arises from the various beasts wanting to know just what the Scroobious Pip is, 'Fish or Insect, or Bird or Beast'. The treetop proves as dissonant as the ground ('the Parrot chattered, the Blackbird sung ... the Peacock began to scream'), and so do the sea ('a splashy, squashy, spluttery sound') and the insect-filled shore with its 'buzztilential Flies'. In response to the endless entreaties for categorization, the Scroobious Pip will only offer sonorous nonsense and a repeat of its name. The reply varies for each audience though remains similar enough on each occasion to work as a refrain to the poem. Using 'a rumbling sound' in response to the land beasts, it sings 'Chippetty Flip – Flippetty Chip – / My only name is the Scroobious Pip'. The first line of the refrain reverses itself into 'Flippetty chip – Chippetty flip', sung with 'a chirpy sound' for the birds; the fish receive the answer 'Plifatty flip – Pliffity flip' delivered with 'a liquid sound', while the insects must settle for 'Wizziby wip – wizziby wip' communicated with 'a whistly sound'.[5]

Here, then, is a particularly sonant poem, yet one whose noise outside of the beasts' world is perhaps not particularly bothersome. On the contrary, sound's potential as pleasure for both speakers and listeners is obvious when the verse is read aloud. As with most successful literature for younger children, there is plenty of opportunity for putting on voices, making silly noises and enjoying the musicality of the words. Beyond this, however, there are also other readings we could apply, for example by attending to the way sounds are matched to different environments. There may not be much to notice between the sound the Pip makes when singing to animals and birds, beyond rumblingness, chirpiness and the tongue-twisting phonemic reversal which takes place between 'chippetty flip' and 'flippetty chip'. But there is something identifiably watery about 'plifatty flip' (which resonates with the watery lisp of Lear's 'thong', 'O Thuthan Thmith! Thweet Thuthan Thmith!') and something buzzy, flighty and insect-like about 'wizziby wip'. Perhaps the Pip is a multilinguistic entity that can communicate to its varied audiences in their native dialects. Or is it that the physical environment affects the Pip's sound box so that we are supposed to imagine 'plifatty' as a voice heard through water and 'wizziby' as the result of melding into the harmonics of the shoreline? Or perhaps each listener hears the sounds they want to hear, making their necessary local translations.

We might choose to hear the poem as a source of sonic pleasure for reciters and listeners, or as a commentary on the inherent foolishness of babble, chatter and buzz, noting that the Owl, alone among the beasts, is presented with the twin signs of wisdom and silence. Either way, we can hear that sound is crucial to the text, both as something being represented by the written words – and hence as inherently nonsensical, given that we don't know these words – and in Lear's attempts at sound writing (phonography).

If Lear's poem offers a translation of sound to writing and vice versa, it also presents, as do so many tales for children, a translation into English of the language of animals, birds, fish and insects. Nor is it, as we might initially think, merely a partial translation, for even the 'foreign' words are designed to be read according to the phonetic strategies employed by speakers of English. In this respect, 'The Scroobious Pip' accords with what Lecercle notes in his reading of Lewis Carroll's 'Jabberwocky', a poem which follows standard linguistic process, including phonetics, morphology, syntax and semantics. Of these qualities, the first three provide little in the way of problems because Carroll's poem 'is eminently readable, an excellent choice for public reading' and, unlike the Gryphon's 'Hjckrrh!', the words all 'conform to the phonotactics of English'.[6] Carroll's language, like Stanley Unwin's Unwinese the following century, is an imitation of English and so sounds fairly 'normal'. But when it comes to semantics, everything falls apart and confusion sets in. Alice responds to the poem by saying that it 'seems very pretty' but *'rather* hard to understand! ... Somehow it seems to fill my head with ideas – only I don't exactly know what they are! However, *somebody* killed *something*: that's clear.'[7] Her response, as Lecercle emphasizes, shows that 'narrative coherence somehow compensates for semantic incoherence'.[8] It may also be that there is something in the music of the poem that communicates sense, a point made by T. S. Eliot in his 1942 essay 'The Music of Poetry'. Eliot describes Lear's nonsense poems as 'a parody of sense', which seems a good way to describe 'Jabberwocky' too.[9] For the parody to work, there must be enough pre-existing sense to recognize a relationship, leading to the seeming paradox faced by Alice wherein a sound text is simultaneously 'hard to understand' and 'clear'.

Carroll showed a repeated interest in the pronunciation of his neologisms, telling the readers of 'Jabberwocky' that 'slithy' should sound like the two words 'sly, the'; that the 'g's in 'gyre' and 'gimble' should be hard; and that 'rath' should rhyme with 'bath' (not that this would completely clarify matters, given the regional variations in English pronunciations of 'bath'). So, while it could easily be argued that the new sounds in 'Scroobious Pip' and 'Jabberwocky' are different types – the former being imitations of actual animal noises and the latter being completely new entities based on combined elements of existing words – the role of the speaker was considered important by both men. As Lecercle argues, 'The world of Wonderland is not mainly about little girls and Jabberwocks, it is about little girls as speakers and Jabberwocks as coinages, that is, as words.' This echoes a point made by Elizabeth Sewell, who writes that the nonsense universe is 'not a universe of things but of words and ways of using them, plus a certain amount of pictorial illustration'.[10] This does not mean we have to go so far as to claim that the sound of the words is more important than their sense; rather, the sense is in the sound, whether in the closeness of Lear's animal imitations to their referents or in the way that Carroll's portmanteau words combine existing meanings: 'slithy' as a compound of 'slimy' and 'lithe', 'frumious' of 'fuming' and 'furious'.

As Sewell highlights, it is not only people who communicate in Carroll's works: 'In the Alices, flowers, insects, animals, legs of mutton, Christmas puddings, playing cards and chessman, can all speak, and the result is that they and Alice are perpetually involved in a particular kind of dialectic.'[11] These are noisy books, filled with conversation; even when Alice is not talking to someone or something else, she is talking to herself. This is no doubt necessary for Carroll to work through the logic games that are at the heart of his nonsense; in classical style, the explication, no matter how befuddling, is facilitated by dialogue and interlocutors. Lear's work, meanwhile, is less about conversation and more about description of people, animals, things, places and events, an emphasis that also informs the nonsense literature of Mervyn Peake and Edward Gorey in the twentieth century.

It has often been suggested that Alice stands in for the reader since she questions the nonsense that comes her way and demands explanations from the other characters, often engaging in frustrating battles of logic which she seems destined to lose. But Alice is also presented by Carroll as an author of nonsense; Wonderland turns out to be her own creation, conjured up in a dream. Throughout the text there are significant examples of Alice-authored nonsense, such as when she considers sending new boots to her distant feet every Christmas with carrier directions that read *'Alice's Right Foot, Esq. / Hearthrug / near the Fender / (with Alice's love)'* (*AA*, 21). On this occasion, she stops herself with the admonition 'Oh dear, what nonsense I'm talking!', while in the same passage, her cry of 'curiouser and curiouser!' is accompanied by an authorial aside noting that Alice 'was so much surprised, that for the moment she quite forgot how to speak good English' (*AA*, 20). As is frequently the case with Alice, there is the simultaneous awareness of propriety and impropriety, a set of dilemmas about how to conduct oneself in the world and the extent to which one can submit to Wonderland whimsy. In terms of sound, it is interesting when reading Carroll to imagine what kind of accent each character has; the tone in which Carroll writes Alice (and writes for Alice) suggests that the propriety of her speech is accompanied by a well-spoken, perhaps rather prim, speaking manner. This effect has subsequently been compounded by audio–visual adaptations of the Alice stories, as we will hear later.

Given the tension between propriety and impropriety in the Alice books, it is perhaps little wonder that the rabbit hole and the looking-glass have been understood in terms of the unconscious. The worlds of sense and nonsense, too, are often presented as being analogous to the rational and irrational or the conscious and the unconscious.

And while it may be argued that there is no clear border between one of these zones and another, this does not seem to prevent our wishing to act as if such borders did exist. This creates the kind of self-checking we witness in the quotations from Carroll mentioned above and accounts for the framing of Carroll's Alice stories within conventional binaries of above and below ground, this and that side of the mirror, the waking and the dreaming mind. From a sonic perspective, it is interesting to listen out for the role sound plays in identifying these zones and in determining the passage between them. This becomes obvious at the close of the first Alice book when, after Alice explains her dream to her sister, the latter recreates the dream in her own mind, guided by an array of sounds:

> So she sat on, with closed eyes, and half believed herself in Wonderland, though she knew she had but to open them again, and all would change to dull reality – the grass would only be rustling in the wind, and the pool rippling to the waving of the reeds – the rattling teacups would change to tinkling sheep-bells, and the Queen's shrill cries to the voice of the shepherd-boy – and the sneeze of the baby, the shriek of the Gryphon, and all the other queer noises, would change (she knew) to the confused clamour of the busy farm-yard – while the lowing of the cattle would take the place of the Mock Turtle's heavy sobs. (*AA*, 126)

The 'queer noises' are those which register impropriety in the Alice books, all the sonic warfare waged upon the well-spoken, well-poised and supposedly well-meaning Alice as she attempts to retain the rational upper hand over her interlocutors. That these noises can switch so easily to those of the clamorous farmyard only reiterates the sense prevalent throughout the stories of animals as Other, and of the animality of otherness more generally. Such bestial raucousness unites Carroll, Lear and other writers of nonsense literature.

At the same time, such texts celebrate the rebellious otherness of noise. In her introduction to Lear's *Complete Nonsense and Other Verse*, Vivien Noakes traces a history of antecedents, including Aristophanes's *The Birds*, Roman Saturnalia, European minstrel traditions, 'the irreverent topsy-turvydom of the Feast of Fools', jesters, mummers' plays, Shakespeare, music halls and circuses. The Victorian era in which Lear lived received all these past moments even as it witnessed a decline in oral culture. Due to this decline, and to the morally and religiously austere atmosphere of the time, Lear's work stood out as a rebellious and glorious throwback to the irreverence of the past. It appeared mostly as text and pictures but relied equally on sounded performance, as Noakes highlights: 'Though now within the pages of a book, the element of performance is retained, created by the conjunction of words and picture. ... The rhythm of the verse is a dance rhythm, but an awkward, big-footed dance, like a rustic jig.'[12]

Rhyme and rhythm, which Jacqueline Flescher recognizes as 'the very stuff of nonsense', are vital aspects of nonsense songs and limericks and provide examples of the sonic logic that provides the framework to the nonsense.[13] Alliteration, which is a particular kind of rhyming–rhythmic device, plays an important role in the way sound orders words in the nonsense text, as in the lines from 'The Walrus and the Carpenter' that tell 'of shoes and ships and sealing-wax / Of cabbages and kings' (*AA*, 185). As Flescher notes, 'once the pattern has been so sharply defined, shoes, ships, and sealing-wax can co-exist happily, and cabbages and kings live side by side'.[14] A kind of normality thus ensues, strengthened in this example by the normalizing power of the list; Francis Spufford, who uses this example for the title of a compendium of lists, writes that these 'five words from different categories of concrete noun ... alliterate as if they sat together by natural dispensation of sound'.[15]

Another way in which alliteration, rhyming and listing combine is in the nonsense alphabet, of which Lear provided examples such as 'A was an ant', 'The Absolutely Abstemious Ass', 'A was an Area Arch' and 'A was once an apple pie'. In the latter (*CN*, 279–304), each verse begins with the same verbal and rhythmic structure: 'A was once an apple pie', 'B was once a little bear', 'C was once a little cake', deviating only when encountering a letter with more than one syllable or whose word provides difficulties for the single-syllable word or the countable noun: 'W was once a whale', 'X was once a great king Xerxes', 'Z was once a piece of zinc'. Variations applied to the opening lines capitulate to the need for real words to be used, whereas the body of the verses show allegiance not to existing vocabulary but to the sonic pleasures of nonsensical rhyming groups that riff on each alphabetical noun: 'apple pie' morphs into 'Pidy / Widy / Tidy / Pidy / Nice insidy'; 'cake' into 'Caky / Baky / Maky / Caky / Taky Caky'; 'goose' into 'Goosy / Moosy / Boosy

/ Goosey / Waddly-woosy'. Like Lear, Edward Gorey was drawn to writing and illustrating nonsense alphabets which likewise play with the possibilities of sonic serialism. *The Gashlycrumb Tinies* (1963) details, in abecedarian form, the grisly undoing of twenty-six children, from 'Amy who fell down the stairs' and 'Basil assaulted by bears' to 'Yorick whose head was knocked in' and 'Zillah who drank too much gin'. *The Utter Zoo* (1967) is an A–Z nonsense bestiary that houses the Ampoo, the Boggerslosh, the Ippagoggy, the Twibbit, on through to the Zote. In the former work, sound plays its most obvious form in the rhyming dactyls; in the latter, there is the pleasure of speaking the beasts' names out loud.

If alliteration, repetition and listing can create structure through their phono-logic, the interruption or testing of this logic is also a much-used nonsense strategy. Lear himself strains the logic of rhythm and rhyme in his work, as Ann Colley notes by highlighting the rhymed pairs 'Coblenz / immense' and 'Prague / plague' that appear in two of his limericks: 'In their haste to correspond, these words trip over each other and expose the stumbling blocks of their individuality. The rhyme is at once completed and broken apart.'[16] In the case of 'There was a Young Lady of Portugal / Whose ideas were excessively nautical', rhythm and rhyme come dangerously close to collapse (*CN*, 163). One is so used to Lear's leading lines resolving on a strong eighth syllable (even in the cases when there are nine syllables, such as 'There was an old Person of Chili') that in mouthing the 'Portugal' limerick, one struggles to find the rhythm. That this is followed by a line of eleven or twelve syllables (depending on one's pronunciation of 'ideas'), including the rhythmically unfriendly 'excessively', only makes recitation of the verse trickier. 'Nautical', meanwhile, may be an example of Colley's non-corresponding pairs but, given the trouble caused by the preceding words, it appears quite fitting, a logical word to put against 'Portugal'.

There is disruption of a different kind in 'The Courtship of Yonghy-Bonghy-Bò' when Lear breaks a word at the end of the line to force a rhyme: 'Though you're such a Hoddy Doddy – / Yet I wished that I could modi- / fy the words I needs must say!' (*CN*, 326). And in the closing couplet of 'Mrs Jaypher Found a Wafer', we find 'For there's nothing half so dread= / =ful, as Lemons in your head!' (*CN*, 448). A 'silent' reading will uncover the jagged, forced nature of these rhymes, no doubt closely followed by an appreciation of them as nonsense strategies, ways of exaggerating the playful aspect of the poem's content. Reading aloud, meanwhile, will cause reciters to adopt a certain rhythmic stress if they wish to communicate the rhyme (and the orthography), encountering a mild verbal rebellion as regular phonology is cast momentarily aside.

'alphybettyformed verbage'

If nonsense literature of the type associated with Carroll and Lear presents us with a relatively intact language system used to describe nonsensical situations, but which itself is occasionally breached by neologisms and light experimentation, much modernist literature provides a far greater challenge when it comes to comprehension of the words on the page. Among the modernists writing in English, James Joyce remains one of the most challenging. In particular, his two epic novels *Ulysses* and *Finnegans Wake* offer ground for endless interpretation, as is shown by the ever-growing body of exegetic literature devoted to them. For our purposes, it is the role of sound in the presentation and understanding of Joyce's experimental style that is of special interest. To take a typical example from *Ulysses*, here is a sentence depicting Leopold Bloom's inner voice responding to the sounds he hears as he passes a school where pupils are learning the alphabet and geography: 'Ahbeesee defeegee kelomen opeecue rustyouvee double you. Boys are they? Inishturk. Inishark. Inishboffin. At their joggerfry. Mine. Slieve Bloom.'[17] The alphabet is learnt as a chant, a mnemonic device, while place names are learnt via phonemic variation – in this case, the Gaelic names of three islands off the coast of Ireland as well as a reference to the Slieve Bloom Mountains. The passage gives up its reliance more obviously when read aloud, as is often the case with Joyce's work.

One of the recurring features of the work is the challenge posed to writer and reader in fixing sound in written form. It is no secret that Joyce made much use of sound in his work, yet he is rightly known as a writer, as one whose formal experiments, however reliant they were on audio–visual elements, ultimately play out on the page. We needn't see this as a paradox, but rather as a vital example of the interconnected workings of seeing, reading, hearing, listening, mouthing and mimesis. To take another example from *Ulysses*, the account of the beach in the third chapter ('Proteus') is particularly notable for multiple reflections on sound in relation to the other senses and on the sensing of time and space. One passage which touches on the nonsensical (while still being fully understandable in the sense-world of the described beach) depicts the soundscape of the shore:

> Listen : a fourworded wavespeech : seesoo, hrss, rsseeiss ooos. Vehement breath of waters amid seasnakes, rearing horses, rocks. In cups of rocks it slops : flop, slop, slap : bounded in barrels. And, spent, its speech ceases. It flows purling, widely flowing, floating foampool, flower unfurling. (*U*, 49)

This is a poetry of sound effects, some more pronounceable than others, words which beg to be read aloud for the way they flow and lap against each other in the mouth. The repeated 'p's' and 'b's' which burst as plosives through the lips, the hiss of the 's's', the alliteration of 'bounded in barrels', 'spent ... speech' and 'flowing, floating foampool, flower unfurling', the rhyme of 'rocks', 'flop', 'slop' and 'slap', of 'purling' and 'unfurling', the bubbling, babbling gerunds. In this chapter, which opens with the 'ineluctable modality of the visible' and which makes multiple references to eyes opening and closing, sound works with sight to conjure up the multisensorial drama of the shoreline.

Many scholars interested in the role of sound – and especially musical sound – in *Ulysses* have focused on the eleventh chapter, 'Sirens'.[18] More than any of its predecessors, this is the chapter where narrative breaks down and is replaced by fragments of conversations, observations, songs and inner musings. Multiple voices are seemingly heard at once – as far as such an effect can ever be achieved in print – as the barmaids of the Ormond Hotel gossip and take orders from patrons, and as the patrons converse, sing and listen to music. As these and other sound effects – including the ever more 'audible' tap-tap-tapping of the blind piano tuner's stick – interweave, the chapter becomes a sonic palimpsest in which the reader is put to work navigating narrative courses through the choppy layers. Alan Shockley writes that the lines of many of the chapter's sentence fragments 'seem more about sound than sense', echoing the distinction famously placed by Carroll in *Alice's Adventures in Wonderland*.[19] Similarly, Jeri Johnson writes of 'Sirens' that

The governing rules here are acoustic, not linguistic. ... The aural logic of the episode – passages spawn other passages through similarities of sound; words arrange themselves into alliterative, mellifluous, cacophonous, rhythmic, assonantal, rhyming patterns; the acoustic voice (as sound) nudges out the graphic mark (as sense) – produces a noisy static profoundly disruptive of narrative coherence.[20]

Such distinctions between sound and sense are something of a commonplace, and we might do well to question them. I am not completely convinced, for example, by Johnson's suggestion (as I read it) that sound is in some way an obstruction to narrative coherence; if anything, it is Joyce's experimental writing that is the greatest obstruction. It would seem more accurate to say that the noisiness of 'Sirens' and other 'phonetic' sections of *Ulysses* provide a narrative consistency, but that semantic content is blocked out in and by the written text.

Consider again Alice's response to 'Jabberwocky', where there is a recognition that something is being related, though some of the details may be unclear. Another way to put this would be to say that a type of sense-making that is sonic (Johnson's 'aural logic') takes over the narrative and our expectations of it. Indeed, as with experimental music which has taken voice(s) as its constituent parts (for example, work by Trevor Wishart, Alvin Lucier, Paul Lansky or Laurie Anderson), we might say that the sonic provides a comfortably (sirenically seductive) coherent narrative despite or due to the loss of sensible words. T. S. Eliot's musings on music and poetry are apposite again here. Wishing to emphasize that 'the music of poetry is not something which exists apart from meaning', Eliot notes that 'there are poems in which we are moved by the music and take the sense for granted, just as there are poems in which we attend to the sense and are moved by the music without noticing it'. Eliot uses Lear as example, claiming that Lear's 'nonsense is not vacuity of sense: it is a parody of sense, and that is the sense of it. *The Jumblies* is a poem of adventure, and of nostalgia for the romance of foreign voyage and exploration; *The Yongy-Bongy Bo* and *The Dong with a Luminous Nose* are poems of unrequited passion – "blues" in fact'.[21] It is important to note that Eliot is discussing poetry as a medium in which sound and music are arguably more prevalent than in prose, yet Joyce is nothing if not a musical prose writer. Even so, sound does not take over entirely in *Ulysses* or in any work where the medium at hand is a written novel. As Jean-Jacques Lecercle says, 'writing outside sense proves to be surprisingly difficult, for meaning puts up a fight', while Jeri Johnson notes that, ultimately, 'Ulysses (and no less *Ulysses*) resists the Sirens' song'.[22]

Hugh Kenner argues that Joyce writes in the voice of his characters rather than as a detached narrator, even though he appears to offer such objective narration. Kenner refers to this as 'the Uncle Charles Principle', after the character in *Portrait of the Artist as a Young Man*.[23] The Spanish novelist Julián Ríos, whose work is heavily influenced by Joyce, takes this idea further in his own epic novel *Larva: Midsummer Night's Babel* by having the characters voice their own opinions of 'Herr Narrator', a 'ventriloquacious nut who misproduces our voices. ... A cunning conning cofounder and confounder. The Echommentator who dubdoubles us and tries to root in black-and-white everything we live and write en route. ... In his deliriums he thinks he's the author of our feuilleton, our surreal serial.'[24] This word stew, typical of Ríos's punning, sense-deferring style, brings together notions of the death of the author, the metaphysics of presence and speech, and, via the mention of 'dub', the manipulation of words through sound technology. As with *Ulysses* and *Finnegans Wake*, the babbling text takes on a life of its own and overflows the sanity of narration. Is this the unconscious speaking, or the sound of language in love with its reproducibility, its tendency towards rhizomatic growth and mutation?

As an earlier 'Echommentator who dubdoubles us and tries to root in black-and-white everything we live and write en route', Joyce made constant reference to the detachments, mutations and mediations provided by twentieth-century sound technology. Phonographic, radiographic and filmic voices can be heard throughout *Ulysses* and *Finnegans Wake* as both explicit references and as dubdoubling techniques to 'root in black-and-white' the fractured nature of modern listening, and of memory and thinking more generally. The phonograph as a technology of memory is evoked in a passage in the 'Hades' chapter of *Ulysses*, as Bloom wonders 'how could you remember everybody?':

> Well, the voice, yes: gramophone. Have a gramophone in every grave or keep it in the house. After dinner on a Sunday. Put on old

greatgrandfather Kraahraark! Hellohellohello amawfullyglad kraark awfullygladaseeragain hellohello amarawf kopthsth. Remind you of the voice like the photograph reminds you of the face. (*U*, 109)

Here Joyce emulates the hesitations, skips, sound effects and obstructive noises of early phonography, suggesting that the medium of recording was another way in which sense might turn to nonsense. Unknowingly, he anticipates the practices of later sound artists such as John Cage, Christian Marclay and John Oswald and of numerous samplers and remixers. A difference, though, would be that recording, when Joyce was working on *Ulysses*, was still relatively primitive and more prone to 'natural' obstructions, whereas artists working in an era of greater technical perfection would choose to deliberately construct glitch, just as Joyce had deliberately mutated prose.[25]

Steven Connor posits *Ulysses* as 'a work of voicing', one that 'anticipates its successor, *Finnegans Wake*, in beginning to use the novel form as a sounding board or receiving apparatus for the manifold voices, styles, and idioms which throng about and permeate modern subjectivity'. He underlines the confusion of a multi-voiced world in which there is too much noise, asking 'who speaks, when everything has a voice?'[26] *Ulysses*, while more coherent as a text than *Finnegans Wake*, is beholden to a wealth of sonic sources drawn from high culture, classical thought, everyday speech, popular culture, folk song, and the hubbub of the natural and urban world.[27] Joyce acts as both receiver and emitter of these sounds: both ends, as it were, of the gramophonic device. With phonography as sound writing in mind, it's possible to suggest that Joyce is fixing these sounds in black and white in a manner that is analogous to the etching of sound into wax. Sometimes the result is unreadable to the human eye, just as the patterns in the groove are unreadable to the needle; sometimes, there is signal interference, glitch, miscommunication. And if this is already a major issue in *Ulysses*, it becomes an almost insurmountable one in *Finnegans Wake*.

Joyce's final novel continues – and amplifies to a quite bewildering extent – the dynamic interplay between written and sounded communication initiated by its predecessor. At times, it seems as if the text can only be understood when read aloud (or better, when one hears an expert reciter recite it); at others, it seems impossible to know how to bring the printed letters to voice. The insistence on sound that resists easy pronunciation – for example, the famous early sentence 'The fall (babadalgharaghtakamminavronnkonnbronntonnerronntuonnthunntrovarrrhounawnskawntoohoohoordenentthurnuk!) of a once wallstrait oldparr is retaled early in bed and later on life down through all Christian minstrelsy' – partakes in what Jean-Jacques Lecercle calls 'the linguistics of *délire*'.[28] In the presence of such a word, one wonders whether, rather than owning language, the author has become possessed by it. As for the reader, it is so much easier in this case to let the eye lazily roll over the word than it is to enact the lingering necessary to say it aloud (go back and try). Yet, as we know from the exegesis, there is 'sense' in Joyce's epic word (it is a conjunction of words for thunder in various languages); and, as we know from audio versions of the text, the word can be sounded, and sounded well (did you manage?). As Lecercle says of Joyce's tongue-twister, 'A "word" like this plays on sounds, and makes it clear that the overall construction of meaning is also obtained by the careful marshalling of sounds, as even the most incompetent poet knows.'[29] Or, as Joseph Campbell and Henry Morton Robinson put it in their mythology-laced commentary, Joyce 'had to smelt the modern dictionary back to protean plasma and re-enact the "genesis and mutation of language" in order to deliver his message. But the final wonder is that such a message could have been delivered at all!'[30]

Finnegans Wake works, even as it forces a mental workout. And it works (out) best when readers are willing to listen to the words on the page and, better, to sing along to Joyce's peculiar solfage ('Don't retch meat fat salt lard sinks down' (*FW*, 260)), relish in his rhythmic alliterations ('Gaunt grey ghostly gossips growing grubber in the glow' (*FW*, 594), 'the hundering blundering dunderfunder of plundersundered manhood' (*FW*, 596)), tip a vocal wink to his punning word play ('Conk a dook he'll do' (*FW*, 595)) and generally be open to the 'variously inflected, differently pronounced, otherwise spelled, changeably meaning vocable scriptsigns' (*FW*, 118). With regard to the vocable scriptsigns, Joyce also offers clues as to how to read-hear-say what he's telling us: 'What can't be coded can be decorded if an ear aye sieze what no eye ere grieved for' (*FW*, 482). These words revel in palindromic play, the sonic palindrome that matches 'ear aye' with 'eye ere'.

For Steven Connor, they may also tell us something about how 'best' to understand the *Wake*: 'the motto seems to advise us that what cannot be deciphered by the eye is available to be at once decoded and recorded by the more retentive and attentive ear.' But as Connor also notes, 'the advantage of the ear may lie precisely in its deficiency, its tendency to associate with other senses'.[31] It is certainly the case that the writing and reading eye asserts authority over the word through spelling, fixing words in ways that mouths and ears may not. Sounds can be a 'phoney habit' (*FW*, 533); undocumented phonemes, no less than telephones and phonographs, may only offer sonic fakery.

The voice slows the eye down. Look at any of the more stream-of-consciousness sections of *Ulysses* (the final chapter for example) or any of *Finnegans Wake*. The eye, dazzled, rushes across the page, wondering at the wash of words but not necessarily taking them all in. Try reading it aloud and a slowing is forced. The eye can always dwell but that dwelling is likely to be accompanied by a greater awareness of the work of inner speech as a way of coming to terms with the flood of words. *Finnegans Wake* is 'an overgrown babeling' (*FW* 6): before and beyond language in its simultaneous under- and over-development; a text bursting with excessive sound and music; a river of words and sounds without beginning or end, infinitely emptying itself into the ocean of language only to be drawn up again as evaporation. It's the book that never runs dry.

'babellicose baabling'

Steven Connor suggests that *Finnegans Wake* is more 'imitable' than *Ulysses*.[32] This seems to be borne out by Julián Ríos's *Larva: Midsummer Night's Babel*, a 1983 novel written in Spanish and translated into English in 1990. Where Ríos's subsequent *Casa Ulises* (2003, translated as *The House of Ulysses* in 2010) is based on the structure of *Ulysses* (which was in turn based on the structure of Homer's *Odyssey*), *Larva* is Wakean to its core. Often, words are only connected to each other by sound, through plays on words which are either homophones or which bear close sonic relationships. In such homophonic instances, meaning is opened out and readers are able to 'get' the relationships between the words. Ríos is an unabashed Joycean and there are many obvious comparisons between his works and Joyce's last two great novels.[33] In addition to the endless word play and general cacophony of the text, Ríos also uses footnotes to an even greater degree than Joyce in *Finnegans Wake*. *Larva* is formatted so that each double-page spread contains the main story on the right-hand page and the footnotes on the left. The use of space and the sense of multiple voices speaking recall not only Joyce but also texts such as Martin Gardner's *Annotated Alice*, Jacques Derrida's *Glas* and Roland Barthes's *S/Z*.

As Connor said of Joyce, Ríos can be seen as a receiver to the world's sound; in an interview, he describes how he came to write *Larva* 'bit by bit, listening to the beating of the words'.[34] At one point in *Larva*, in an echo of Dante, we are told about 'babellicose baabling, diverse lingue, orribili favelle ..., and scraps of misheard mumblings'.[35] Like Joyce, Ríos has the tendency to incorporate into his text the surreal and/or everyday narratives of literary, artistic and political figures such as Napoleon, Don Juan, Don Quixote and Sinbad, a legacy which can be traced further back to Rabelais, another of Ríos's main influences. 'I hold the liberation theory', Ríos quips, 'that the best writers liberate the language from taboos, tattoos, cockatoos, repetitions, old fashion repressions and expressions, clichés, fetters, and so forth. For this reason I call it sometimes liberature for short, this liberating literature'.[36] Furthermore, like Joyce, Ríos revels in sound and music references, though as a more recent author, he has a whole range of vernacular examples that Joyce would not have known (one double-page is devoted to plays on the words 'rock' and 'roll'). As with other writers mentioned in this chapter, Ríos shows how the sound of nonsense can inform and animate the words of the page, encouraging readers to approach the text as transcription and score.

Audio

So far, this chapter has been considering the role of sound in the workings of nonsense as it exists on the page. In the case of the classic nonsense texts of Lear and Carroll, we recognize that the texts, while oral in origin, have become canonized in the forms in which they appear in print. In the case of Joyce and Ríos, we witness writers acutely tuned-in to the sounds of everyday life and language but whose work, again, has been 'frozen' in text. Yet these writers have produced work which is not only read silently, but which is brought to noisy life in recitations and adaptations. At the outset of *Alice in Wonderland*, Alice famously questions the point of a book without pictures and conversations. The book in question is being read by her sister, presumably in silence. How might Alice feel about a book that the reader doesn't need to peep into at all, a book whose conversations and pictures can be heard? In the decade following the publication of the Alice stories, such a possibility would be realized with the advent of recorded sound and the subsequent possibility of detaching story from storyteller and making books audible. From Edison's recording of 'Mary Had a Little Lamb' in 1877 and a showcase recording of 'Hey Diddle Diddle, the Cat and the Fiddle' the following year, a recording industry developed that sought to preserve the spoken word and to add new dimensions to it.[37] Not surprisingly, literature for children constituted a significant proportion of what would come to be known as audiobooks.

There have been countless sonic adaptations of the Alice stories in many languages. Among these is a 1958 recording on pioneering spoken-word label Argo of an adaptation by BBC Radio producer Douglas Cleverdon. The story is narrated by Margaretta Scott and stars the twelve-year-old Jane Asher as Alice. The voices are much as one might expect of a recording of this vintage, crystal-clear 'BBC' accents. This makes it seem like everything being related is absolutely normal, the voices acting as a kind of suture between the enunciated and the enunciation. Such was clearly the intention, as the liner notes to the recording use 'no-nonsense' as a description of Alice and make it clear that this aspect of her character was being aimed for in the adaptation.[38]

This is useful because it makes manifest something which is already there in Carroll's text, what we might call the child's resistance to nonsense. It goes largely unquestioned that nonsense literature, while appealing to adults, is primarily designed for children and that children make the ideal audience due to their 'childishness', a set of qualities which are hard to define precisely but which might include curiosity, imagination, a heightened sense of play and inexperience, the latter compensated partly by an inventiveness alloyed to learning. Less discussed is the exaggerated seriousness with which children occasionally resist the nonsensical and demand explanations better suited to the logical aspects of what they are learning about the world and about comporting themselves as human beings. In contrast to the endless play of nonsense, then, we might note an attitude within the child that could indeed be described as 'no-nonsense'. This seems an apt description of Alice as she is presented in Carroll's texts, persistently resistant to the nonsense she finds surrounding her in Wonderland but concerned about its viral possibility.

If Cleverdon's recording sounds staid to contemporary ears, there are nevertheless moments of sonic weirdness. The earliest comes in the first track, 'Down the Rabbit Hole', as Alice asks herself 'Do cats eat bats? Do bats eat cats?' Cleverdon's production adds repetitions of this with echo and fading, a sonic addition that acts as a supplement to the written text. When words are repeated in this manner, especially single-syllable words presented in alternating patterns, we are alerted to the drift between sense and nonsense, with words becoming babble or music.[39] Another drift from no-nonsense narration to sonic experimentation comes in the 'Pig and Pepper' section, where the noises emitted by the Fish-Footman and the Frog-Footman as they bow into each other mix into a bubbling, babbling incoherence. Elsewhere, in 'Advice from a Caterpillar' for example, the sound of nonsense is elevated by the simple removal of the names of characters and reporting verbs that are necessary sense-making tools in the written text. So, instead of 'Alice hastily replied', we hear Alice's hasty reply without intervention from Scott as narrator. Voices alert us to who is speaking and we are placed as witnesses to the absurd conversational tennis being played by Alice and the Caterpillar. Only when the plot needs to proceed in this abridged version does Scott's voice again enter to reorient the listener. The effect of the conversational sections is akin to the plays of Samuel Beckett, with their famous absurdist sparring between characters (Estragon and Vladimir, Hamm and Clov, Winnie and Willie).

Movies, presumably, would have appealed to Alice, replete as they are with pictures and conversations. There have been many film adaptations of the Alice stories, from Percy Stow and Cecil Hepworth's 1903 version onward, allowing further consideration of how Wonderland and Looking-Glass Land sound.[40] Particularly notable is the soundtrack to Jonathan Miller's unusual adaptation for the BBC in 1966. Miller presents the story as a dark psychodrama for adults rather than children. Eschewing the usual technique of having actors dress up as animals, Miller's cast all appear in Victorian dress as human equivalents of Carroll's characters. The often abstract detachment of the characters – especially Alice, who appears, in Paul Mavis's words, 'like a ghost from Henry James rather than ... a spunky, cheerful, delightfully confused little girl' – is enhanced through moody black-and-white film, odd camera angles, asylum-like settings and a general sense of disturbance.[41] The effect is further created by a soundtrack which mixes the ominous – buzzing flies, chattering busy bodies, whispers and echoes – with the exotic in the form of original music by Ravi Shankar. Ominous sounds also dominate in Jan Švankmajer's *Něco z Alenky* (*Alice*, 1987), a mix of live action and animation that, in Clare Kitson's words, is 'more Prague than Oxfordshire'. Kitson notes the 'alarmingly magnified sound effects' in the film, and it's certainly true that the sound creates an unnerving narrative throughout: ticking clocks and watches, dropped and free-falling objects, hard surfaces and liquid splashes, creaking floors and machinery, rustling leaves, smashed glass, splitting clothes and stuffed animals, buzzing insects and screeching beasts (one of which is also a baby).[42] Švankmajer's film, like Miller's, is atypical but deserves highlighting as an authentic response to the subversive aspects of Carroll's nonsense, its proto-surrealism.

Another uncanny take on Alice can be found in an adaptation by composer Randy Greif, released in parts from 1991 to 1993. Greif's *Alice in Wonderland* uses an LP-based audiobook as the basis for a six-hour sound work in which the original audio is sampled, distorted, cut up, phased and otherwise manipulated and mixed with Greif's additional music. Where audio recordings of the Alice stories have tended to emphasize the lighter side of Carroll's nonsense, Greif's version, like Miller's and Švankmajer's films, focuses on the dark and dreamlike aspects of the story. Furthermore, where audiobooks understandably concentrate on delivering the narrative in a timely and practical ('no-nonsense') manner, Greif, as an experimental sound artist, is free to slow the narrative considerably and to explore particular moments in it for hidden depths. This leads to an extra layer of nonsense as the listener is forced to remember where they are in the story following each return from Greif's sonic deviations. Greif explains that he faced a delicate balancing act between fidelity to the original story and his creative ambitions:

I attempted to use the speech in three distinct ways. Firstly, in a traditional manner of storytelling with the music as background, although the music being far more experimental than typical. Secondly, to cut the speech into patterns that would intertwine with the music in order to force it into the mould of a song structure. So that the spoken words would operate as lyrics, without melody, of course, but rhythmically. Finally, to deconstruct the speech itself into abstraction, cutting the words into phonemes, or altering the voice electronically to the extent it becomes purely sound. The tricky part for me was to try to use these three methods of dealing with the text and still not lose sight of the story itself. I wanted the piece to move through cycles from clear story-telling to pure abstraction and then back again.[43]

The move away from 'clear story-telling' becomes prominent at track 4 ('She looked down at her feet'), which includes a repeated sample of Alice saying 'what nonsense I'm talking'. On track 6 ('How doth the little crocodile?'), speech breaks down into unrecognizable sound fragments, encouraging a grasping after meaning, before gradually coming back into focus for the close of the track.[44]

As with Carroll, there are new dimensions to be found in listening to sound recordings of Joyce's work. In the case of *Finnegans Wake*, the sense created by listening may even be greater than that allowed by the printed word. While there isn't the same possibility to linger as there is with the written word, there is, in a good reading, a better sense of flow. Added to this, readings performed with an Irish accent help to place the text (back) in context. One of the best places to start is with Joyce's own recording, made in 1929 by the linguist Charles Kay Ogden in the studio of the Orthological Society in Cambridge. Joyce only reads three pages of the text (*FW*, 213–16), taking just under nine minutes to do so, yet the passage is one of the most famous and popular: the end of the 'Anna Livia Plurabelle' chapter.[45] Joyce's reading – in which he channels his imagined Dublin washerwomen – has a seductive musicality to it that both makes and evades common sense. The lilt, the rhythm and the phonotactics of the reading help to bring out some of the obscure wordplay of the text and clarify how certain words are to be pronounced, where the stress of the sentence is and so on. But, as with the voice of the Sirens, the ear is pleased to such an extent that the listener may go for several seconds (perhaps all nine minutes) without following the 'story'. The listener might feel, like Alice following the recitation of 'Jabberwocky', that the story 'seems very pretty' but *'rather* hard to understand', that 'it seems to fill my head with ideas – only I don't exactly know what they are' (*AA*, 150). As suggested in the liner notes to a 1959 Caedmon recording of *Finnegans Wake* (with Siobhan McKenna reading 'Anna Livia Plurabelle' and Cyril Cusack reading 'Shem The Penman'), 'Joyce reduces language to pure music; and, hearing it, one slips into a kind of swoon, not even listening for words, but only the ebb and flow of sound. The reading-aloud is not one more tool to help penetrate the jungle, but part of the text.'[46] Even so, audio versions make clear that sound is at the heart of any (non) sense-making of this challenging text and suggest that the hypnotic flow is in phenomenological tension with a grasping for meaning; one can't quite abolish the other.

Other recordings of Joyce have included music as a way of complementing the musicality of the text. Patrick Ball's reading, accompanied by his Celtic harp, again shows how many of the sentences become differently evocative when heard than when read. Ball is also adept at bringing out the Irish tonality of Joyce's tall tale; his rendering of the 't's' in 'Tilling a teel of a tum, telling a toll of a teary turty Taubling' (*FW*, 7) reminds the listener/reader of the Irish pronunciation of the 'th' sound while providing an echo of the 'tricky trochees' that appear on the same page of the *Wake* (*FW*, 7). There are numerous other references to troublesome sounds, as when Shem is heard 'hiccupping, apparently impromptued by the hibat he had with his glottal stop, that he kukkakould flowrish' (*FW*, 171); here Ball makes explicit the use of what Marc Shell calls 'stutter writing'.[47] Additionally, Ball's reading alerts listeners to the repeated rhymes for 'Finnegan' that are sprinkled through the text, for example 'fined again' (*FW*, 5) and 'din again' (*FW*, 6). Hearing Ball reading the Shem section is not unlike listening to Stanley Unwin, a similar mixture of sense and unsense, delivered with an assurance that it all really makes perfect sense. And it does, for the recording delivers an ideal iteration of the text – this seems to be how *Finnegans Wake* should sound.[48]

Given the musicality of Joyce's writing and its unshackling of words from easy semantic communication, it is not surprising that many musicians have been drawn to it. Among the early musical adaptations of *Finnegans Wake* are the setting made by John Cage of page 556 as 'The Wonderful Widow of Eighteen Springs' in 1942 (Cage returned to another page on the same page for his 1984 composition 'Nowth upon Nacht'). Harry Partch used the same page as the basis for his composition 'Isobel' and the opening to page 104 for 'Annah the Allmaziful'; both pieces were composed in 1944 and recorded the following year. In 1958, Luciano Berio used the 'Sirens' chapter of *Ulysses* as the basis for 'Thema (Omaggio A Joyce)', an uncanny electronic mix of murky, half-caught readings by Cathy Berberian.[49] André Hodeir composed a 'jazz cantata' entitled *Anna Livia Plurabelle*, which was recorded in 1966; it sets the Anna Livia chapter to a jazz chamber setting, with two singers – Monique Aldebert and Nicole Croisille – delivering the washerwomen's river of words as a kind of jive language. This sets up an intriguing correspondence between Joyce's text and jazz vocabulary – especially on lines such as 'shake it up, do, do!' – while also serving as a reminder of Joyce's indebtedness to song in his writing.[50] The mix of Joyce and jazz vocalese somehow anticipates the work of Van Morrison, who was not averse in his songs to namechecking his Irish forebear. Elsewhere in the sphere of popular music, Kate Bush based her song 'The Sensual World' on a soliloquy by Molly Bloom in *Ulysses*. When she failed to get permission to use Joyce's words for the song, she replaced them with her own, but a later recording (as 'Flower of the Mountain') reinstates Molly's actual speech. If Bush's song(s) render Joyce as pure voice, DJ Spooky's remix of Joyce's recording of 'Anna Livia' brings an already fragmented text into the world of the twenty-first-century remix. Crystal Castles' 2007 single 'Air War', likewise, incorporates 'Sirens' into new sonic textures by way of the group's own chiptune aesthetics and Berio's electronic trickery.[51]

3

Silly Noises

As we saw in Chapter 1, distinctions have often been made between nonsense and gibberish. Noel Malcolm, for example, argues that the only 'trick' that gibberish can achieve is 'to make funny noises'. He suggests that gibberish offers such a highly concentrated form of nonsense language that 'it must dilute itself with words (or at least recognisable vestiges of words) which are not nonsense' in order to be categorized as nonsense.[1] Similarly, the imitation of non-human sounds or incorrectly understood human sounds (for example, the aping of a foreign language which one doesn't understand) might be heard as only producing 'funny noises'. While I'm less concerned with policing the boundaries of 'proper nonsense', I want to retain the suggestion of a sliding scale in which the presence of words oscillates gibberish between sense and lack of sense. Somewhere in those border areas which I'm leaving unpoliced, there resides the nonsense moment, the point of bewilderment that lies between different worlds of meaning. Even if we can't always pin this moment down – for it occurs at different times, speeds and points for different people – it is still rewarding to observe the comings and goings between the seemingly separate spheres of understandable words, 'vestiges of words' and 'funny noises' and to explore the ways they mean to mean.

Sound poetry

The world of sound poetry offers an extreme case for testing the peregrinations of words and other noises, focused as it is on experimental vocal techniques and technologies. As Brandon LaBelle writes, 'sound poetry can be heard as a vital catalog of the choreographies of the mouth'.[2] This inevitably brings up distinctions between sound and sense that are even stronger than those customarily attached to nonsense literature. Composer and vocalist Jaap Blonk defines sound poetry simply as 'poetry where the sound is more important than the meaning, and sometimes there is no meaning at all'.[3] Meaning, here, clearly refers to semantic meaning, and it is true that much, if not most, sound poetry does away with semantics in favour of sonic experimentation. To say that sound poetry has no meaning, then, is akin to saying that music has no meaning, whereas we might prefer to think of sound art and music as engaging in other kinds of (extra-semantic) meaning. As will hopefully be apparent from some of the examples highlighted below, sound poetry has many affiliations with music and it is not uncommon to find sound poetry being chanted or taking its inspiration from musical languages and structures. In addition to addressing this musical connection, I also discuss sound poetry in relation to sound art more generally and, because the sonic play employed by the Dadaists in particular has influenced a range of popular culture, I also reflect on plunderphonics and remix culture.

In a useful overview of sound poetry, Steve McCaffery identifies three phases or 'areas' of relevance, the first of which has no discernible origin but takes in 'archaic and primitive poetries' employing incantation and 'deliberate lexical distortions'. McCaffery's second phase covers the 'diverse and revolutionary investigations into language's non-semantic, acoustic properties' undertaken by the Russian and Italian Futurists and by the Dadaists of Zurich, Berlin and elsewhere. The third phase, which dates mainly from the 1950s onwards and which more obviously accompanies new discoveries made possible by tape and microphone technologies, consists of explorations into 'the micro particulars of morphology, investigating the full expressive range of predenotative forms: grunts, howls, shrieks, etc.'[4] Given the tighter scope of the second and third areas, I will stick with these in what follows.

Known as the architect of Italian Futurism, Filippo Tommaso Marinetti was, along with Luigi Russolo, associated with many of the manifestoes and art events of that movement that were focused on sound, notably Marinetti's concept of *parole in libertà* ('words in freedom') and Russolo's manifesto *L'arte dei Rumori* ('The Art of Noises'). In his major work *Zang Tumb Tumb*, Marinetti sought to echo the sounds of modern life, in particular the machinery, explosions and gunfire of war. In its reliance on onomatopoeia and other attempts to represent sound, the text does away with conventional words and syntax while also utilizing innovative typography to 'free' the words even further. Writing in 1919, Roman Jakobson argued that, for all their positing of new poetic approaches, Marinetti and his fellow Italians had not exploited the sonic potential of language to develop a really new poetry. Rather, Jakobson saw this work as 'a reform in the field of reportage, not in poetic language'.[5] For examples of the latter, he looked to his fellow Russians Velimir Khlebnikov and Alexei Kruchenykh. Jakobson admiringly quotes Kruchenykh's assertion that 'once there is new form it follows that there is new content. ... It is not new subject matter that defines genuine innovation.'[6] Rather than attempt to transcribe the new world with old methods, better to develop new words to speak of past, present and future. Khlebnikov's poetry exemplifies this through its use of words which seem to grow out of each other, or out of the roots and shoots of morphemes. His most famous poem, 'Zaklyatie Smekhom' ('Incantation by Laughter'), is structured around variations on the word *smek* (laugh) in an experiment that both echoes the uncontrollable act of laughing and suggests an infinite range of neologisms based on morphemic mutation. As Nancy Perloff notes, 'the repetition of the sounds *smekh*, *smei*, and *smesh* in different neologisms and of phonemes *kh*, *i*, *sh*, *ch*, *k* mimics the repetitive, sometimes abrasive sound of laughter. Far from creating nonsense, the overabundant contexts for the core referent overdetermine its meaning.'[7]

Due to its abandonment of standard Russian, 'Incantation by Laughter' extends the usual possibilities open to the translator. Gary Kern supplements his 1975 translation with a range of alternative versions, which nevertheless follow a standard pattern of variation; where his principal version uses the lines 'O laugh it out, you laughsters!' and 'Laughify, laughicate, laugholets, laugholets', one of his alternatives offers 'O guff it out, you guffsters' and 'Guffify, gufficate, guffolets, guffolets'. Two decades later, Paul Schmidt takes a different approach, reducing the familiarity of the language further by rendering Khlebnikov's opening line as 'Hlaha! Uthlofan, lauflings!' and a subsequent line as 'Hlaha! Loufenish lauflings lafe, hlohan utlaufly!'[8] Citing Schmidt's version, Marnie Parsons notes how he 'has clearly moved into an area of English equivalent to the realm of Russian, which Khlebnikov opened'. To translate this poem is not so much to strive for literalness, but rather to show fidelity to Khlebnikov's linguistic play, to 'infuse the host language with a similar spirit of malleability'.[9] This flexibility was at the heart of *zaum*, the poetic concept developed by Khlebnikov and Kruchenykh between 1912 and 1913. The word derives from 'za', meaning 'beyond', and 'um', translated as 'mind', 'reason' or 'sense'. Various translations have been posited for *zaum*, including 'transmental', 'trans-rational' and 'trans-sense'. *Zaum* scholar Gerald Janacek suggests that Paul Schmidt's 'beyonsense' remains 'the cleverest and best rendering', given its homophonic similarity to 'nonsense' combined with the expansion rather than negation of sense.[10]

Elaborating on the use of 'za' in *zaum*, Janecek writes, 'in a topographical sense it means "beyond, on the other side of," and by extension "outside of" or "beyond the bounds of." It is a matter of escaping from or going beyond the limits of a locale, in this case of something like rational, intelligible discourse'.[11] In Khlebnikov's own (Schmidt-translated) words,

> Beyonsense language means language situated beyond the boundaries of ordinary reason, just as we say 'beyond the river' or 'beyond the sea'. Beyonsense language is used in charms and incantations, where it dominates and displaces the language of sense, and this shows that it has a special power over human consciousness, a special right to exist alongside the language of reason.[12]

The connection of beyonsense to charms and incantations is another reminder that the *zaum* poets were fascinated by the past of folklore and 'primitive' language, in contrast to Marinetti and the Italian Futurists. In this, they were closer to the Dadaists Hugo Ball and Raoul Hausmann and to the Dada-affiliated Kurt Schwitters. For Ball, *Verse ohne Worte* (poems without words) or *Lautgedichte* (sound poems) were 'devices for inducing the dada state of mind'.[13] Much like mantras where the repetition of magical words is affective, moving someone or something from one state (of consciousness) to another, so Ball wished 'to totally renounce the language that journalism has abused and corrupted' and 'return to the innermost alchemy of the word' and 'even give up the word too, to keep for poetry its last and holiest refuge'.[14]

Dressed like an 'obelisk' and donning 'a high, blue-and-white-striped witch doctor's hat', Ball took to the stage of the Cabaret Voltaire in June 1916 to declaim his sound poems, beginning with 'gadji beri bimba / glandridi lauli lonni cadori' and continuing with 'Labadas gesang and die Wolken' and 'Elefantenkarawane'. The performance proved overwhelming for poet and audience and, 'bathed in sweat', Ball 'was carried down off the stage like a magical bishop'.[15] Much reported, this event has become something of a primal scene for the performance of sound poetry over the last century. The references to shamanism, religion, trance and madness secure Ball's *Lautgedichte* to ritualistic, folkloric processes. So too with Kurt Schwitters's *Ursonate* or *Sonate in Urlauten* (sonata in primordial sounds), written and revised during the 1920s. The opening line of the poem – 'Fumms bö wö tää zää Uu, pögiff, kwii Ee' – is sourced from two poems by Dadaist Raoul Hausmann; Schwitters then extends this Dada-homage into an epic sonic exploration. The structuring principle, as evident from the title, is musical and the poem's destiny as a work to be performed has been assured through many live and recorded performances, by Schwitters himself, his son Ernst, Christopher Butterfield, Jaap Blonk, Christian Bök and many more.[16]

Tape Voices

While Ball, Schwitters and Richard Huelsenbeck helped to launch the sound poem as performance art, the tendency was taken to more vocally ambitious stages by poets such as Henri Chopin, François Dufrêne and Bob Cobbing. Chopin was important not only as an innovator in sound art, but also as a theorist and curator. Between 1958 and 1974, his magazines *Cinquième Saison* and *OU* published a range of experimental poetry in print and as sound recordings, collecting work by Gil Wolman, François Dufrêne, Bernard Heidsieck, Raoul Hausmann, William Burroughs, Brion Gysin and Bob Cobbing among others. Chopin's work, like that of Wolman and Dufrêne, marked an engagement with new sound recording technologies – particularly the tape recorder and microphone – that had not been available to the Dadaists or Futurists. This allowed for the dissection and manipulation of the voice through the isolation of vocal 'microparticles' and for dubbing, splicing, pitch-shifting and otherwise altering what the microphone had captured. Poets could now, in Chopin's words, 'discover the bone structure of the word, the alphabet, that lurks in the verbal spaces'.[17]

Chopin's tape works evolved from pieces in which language gives way to sound to pieces in which unidentifiable sound dominates but from which snatches of language occasionally escape. The 1956 recording of 'Rouge' provides an example of the former type. The word 'rouge' is repeated over and over, along with a limited range of words and short phrases. After about a minute and a half, the rolled 'r' of 'rouge' and the morpheme 'je' (sounded like the French word for 'I') become the predominant sounds. Shortly before the two-minute mark, separate recordings of 'rouge' start to overlap so that each begins before the other has elapsed. The rolled 'r' then becomes less obviously a phoneme and starts to sound more like an engine being revved (for example, on a motorbike or chainsaw), while 'je' becomes more and more pronounced. In the last section of the three-minute piece, all the sounds start to blur together, still sounding like an engine but now more like a food blender; by the end, the 'bone structure' of the word has been ground to mush.[18] By contrast, a longer three-part work from 1966 which goes under the title 'Le Corps' and 'Le Corpsbis' starts out with already manipulated sound which resembles bird song more than human speech (by this point, Chopin was working with microphones in his nose and throat to capture the passage of air through the body). As the piece unfolds, and particularly during its second and third sections, occasional words or parts of words become audible. Rather than the grinding down of language that occurs in 'Rouge', here language figures as an emergence from a prior state of pre-semantic sound.[19]

Cobbing's *ABC in Sound*, completed in 1964 and published the following year as a book and a sound recording, was an experimental work which took each letter of the alphabet as the starting point for a sonic excursion into words from various existing languages as well as neologisms. The first word of 'A', appropriately, is 'Adventure', quickly followed by variations that shift between English and French: 'Aventure / Aventureux ... Aventureuse / Adventurous / A l'aventure'. 'D' is given over to Japanese gibberish – 'Da dageki daha dai dai daido / Daigo-tettei dai-itchakushu' –

while 'Z' is positively polyglottal: 'Ziska zither zloty zenithal / Zen zeppelin Zarathustra zebu / Zend-avesta zephaniah zion'. Other sections play on the sound of letters' names, for example 'N / Ndue / Ndemic', 'O / O A S / O A S I' and 'Q / Kew / Queue / Cue / Q / Coo!'[20] The last example is interesting in that it is clever on the page but doesn't quite work as a sound poem; until the final word, it merely sounds like the letter 'Q' is being repeated (the 'coo' does, however, allow for the repeated sounds to be heard as the imitation of a bird). Cobbing was as interested in the look as the sound of poems, and *ABC in Sound*, like many of his works, uses varied typography as part of its overall design. The printed poem as score offers suggestions for its performance, and Cobbing provides additional guidelines in the published version which partly clarify and partly obscure matters:

> H. Monotonously rhythmical, louder in the middle.
> I. Needle sharp.
> J. Rising to Jubilaire. central section insistent, rising again to Jubilante.
> K. Slower subtle Rhythm.
> L. Sudden accent on Loop, Bleep, Droop. Dedicated to Bill Butler.
> M. Groups of 4 & 3. Dedicated to George Macbeth.[21]

Although not part of the sound performance, these instructions lend themselves to being read aloud, possessing an eerie hypnotic quality not unlike the Shipping Forecast broadcast on the BBC. Cobbing recorded a version of the poem – running to more than twenty minutes – for one side of an LP released in 1965 and again for the BBC's Radiophonic Workshop under the direction of Delia Derbyshire. The first version was a straight reading by Cobbing, while the second employed the sound editing techniques that the Radiophonic team were known for, adding an extra dimension to the sonic adventure.[22]

In addition to his sound and concrete poetry, Cobbing was a prolific organizer of art events and publications. As a theorist, he contributed many reflections on the role and art of poetry as a social, political and community practice. He used the communicative potential of poetry as a way of enacting collective experience, with the body acting as a mediator between individual and group:

Communication is primarily a muscular activity. It is potentially stronger than everyday speech, richer than those monotonous seeming printed words on the page. ... Say 'soma haoma'. Dull. Say it dwelling on the quality of the sounds. Better. Let it say itself through you. Let it sing itself through you. The vowels have their pitch, the phrase has potential rhythms. You do it with the whole of you, muscular movement, voice, lungs, limbs. Poetry is a physical thing. The body is liberated. Bodies join in song and movement. A ritual ensues.[23]

Cobbing's focus on liberation and ritual connects him to other artists and theorists discussed in this book, while his use of 'dwelling' is also pertinent, with its suggestion that the mouth can be hospitable or inhospitable to sounds. Indeed, given the reference to lungs and muscles, there is a more general connection to the bodily aspects of language and of the body as a place for sounds to dwell. We might think here of Gaston Bachelard's connection of poetry and space which likewise highlights dwelling, or of Brandon LaBelle's articulation of the ways in which sonic nonsense emphasizes language, body and materiality:

> Gibberish may be heard as the instantiation of the particular pleasures of having words in the mouth, and all the excitations of self-sounding: to feel the passing of breath as it rises up from within to fill the throat and mouth, conditioned and contoured by the larynx, the muscular force of the tongue moving back and forth, to the final drop into the lips, as sudden energy flows over to reverberate behind the ears, along the skin, and within the environment around. All such movements underscore the voice as an assemblage of signification *and* the corporeal, reminding [us] of the material poetics of language.[24]

While LaBelle makes this observation in a discussion of sound poetry, his and Cobbing's underscoring of the pleasures of vocal sounding might equally be applied to singers, particularly those whose technique involves protracted dwelling on particular words and parts of words. I'm thinking here particularly of the extreme examples one hears in the singing of Björk, Diamanda Galás and Sheila Chandra, though I might hear something similar in jazz singing, soul, R&B or traditional song. It is interesting, for example, to compare versions of the old folk song 'O Death' by traditionalist singers such as Ralph Stanley or Tim Eriksen with that performed by avant-garde vocalist Diamanda Galás. Across the singing of these three artists, we see a loosening of emphasis on the semantic. With Stanley, there is already quite extensive dwelling on certain words, but this is greatly exaggerated by Eriksen; in Galás, not only are these sounds extended to even greater lengths, but the incorporation of a more staccato delivery in the song's verses finds certain words being cast aside as troublesome obstacles en route to what, for Galás, are the key sounds: the words 'O' and 'Death' and a host of non-semantic noises.[25]

The relationship between sound poetry and verbal music arises constantly, often leading to a blurring between artistic worlds. Henri Chopin was keen to remind interviewers that he identified first as a poet, even though his career took him into the world of sound art; Jaap Blonk, meanwhile, reminds his listeners that he is primarily a composer, albeit one known for virtuosic renditions of classic sound poems from the Dadaists onwards. The Canadian artist Paul Dutton refers to what he does as 'soundsinging' as a way of bringing music and sound poetry together. This blurring can equally be heard on the compilation *Carnivocal: A Celebration of Sound Poetry*, where many of the contributions – including Dutton's 'Snare, Kick, Rack, and Floor' – refer to, or even sound like, popular music, for example bpNichol's 'Pome Poem', bill bissett's 'Opening Chant' and Stephen Cain's 'Alph Bites, A Primer'.[26]

Speech Music

Jaap Blonk has explored the blending of words into music with his group Braaxtaal, which features Blonk on voice and saxophone, Rob Daenen on synthesizer and Theo Bodewes on percussion. The group's 1997 piece 'Muzikaret' consists of Blonk intoning the names of instruments used in gamelan orchestras, then stretching the words by either applying extreme vocalization techniques or adding syllables to the basic word. The piece, which runs to over twelve minutes, is made up of a repeated list of instruments: 'suling gambangkayu ketuk genderpanembungbuzz bonagbarung kempyang kendangbatangan ketuk celempung bedug gongagung rebab'.[27] The first and last word of the list is altered on each iteration through elongation: Blonk sings 'suling' in a high, keening register which, as the two syllables are stretched further each time, emulates the sound of the bamboo flute; in contrast, he utilizes throat-singing for 'rebab', making the still-distinct syllables into extended crackles, croaks and buzzes of vocal grit. Here, the word-sense loses out to what would normally be avoided for sense-making and the body's pre- and post-voice sounding apparatuses dominate in a realm beyond words.[28] The intervening words in the gamelan list are altered by the gradual addition of syllables on each iteration; 'ketuk' becomes 'ketuktuk', 'ketuktuktuk', and so on; 'kempyang' eventually transforms to 'kempyangpyangpyangpyangpyangpyangpyangpyangpyangpyangpyangpyangpyangpyangpyangpyang'. Blonk applies a different vocal attack, melody and tone to each word in the list, at times echoing the soft percussive elements of the gamelan, at others the resonance of its suspended gongs. The overall effect of the piece is to seduce the listener into an ever-widening swirl of sound which, due to the lulling effect of the close-miked vocals, enhances the silence surrounding the sounds; as the last crackles of throat noise on the final 'rebab' bring 'Muzikaret' to an end, the silence is tangible.

While in many ways a different type of piece, 'Muzikaret' recalls aspects of Alvin Lucier's classic voice and tape composition *I Am Sitting in a Room* (1969). For that work, Lucier had recorded a text in which he described himself sitting in a room recording the text and explaining what he was going to do next. That involved playing the tape back in the same room and recording it again, and repeating this 'until the resonant frequencies of the room reinforce themselves so that any semblance of my speech, with perhaps the exception of rhythm is destroyed'. With each recording (there are thirty-two repetitions in total) the resonance of the room builds until its frequencies do indeed overwhelm the voice, which becomes an aquatic wash of sound. There is no obvious point at which the voice's ability to communicate clearly cuts off, just a gradual ebbing away of the vocal parts necessary for faithful perception. But because the transition is so gradual the listener can seem to 'hear' Lucier's words even when only their rhythm remains. For Nicolas Collins, Lucier's piece 'frees the voice from the restraint of song and makes a truly new music'. Collins's justification for this claim is that 'speech is the voice unbound, timbrely rich and thick with meaning. Song, on the other hand, forces the voice into narrow norms, stressing rules of tonality, rhythm, texture, and content that have little to do with any language.'[29] I am not so sure; surely it depends what kind of song one is thinking about. While classical song might bind the voice to particular rules, speech too is bound by phonological norms; if anything presents the voice unbound, it is more likely the wilder end of sound poetry. Rather, I would argue that song frees voice from the burden of communicating sense. But for the purposes of this book, I am more interested in that unlocatable moment of transition and bewilderment – that nonsense moment – when the listener is not quite sure whether she is hearing speech or song. Lucier's work exemplifies Henri Chopin's notion that 'on the far side of the alphabet, no more hidden behind script, we encounter the voice, its grain, its ruggedness, its prosodies ... Where new resonances are born'.[30] There is also Bob Cobbing's observation that 'the tape-recorder, by its ability to amplify and superimpose, and to slow down the vibrations, has enabled us to rediscover the possibilities of the human voice, until it becomes again something we can almost see and touch'.[31] *I Am Sitting in a Room* achieves such vocal tangibility, even as the voice itself – what we would normally know as the voice – disappears.

Paul Lansky's 'Idle Chatter' (1985) similarly works around the blurring of incoherent speech and music. Lansky writes, 'To my ear speech and song are not mutually exclusive: there is music in speech and speech in song.' He heightens our awareness of the relationship by manipulating Hannah MacKay's voice so that it veers between comprehensible speech and something more musical. The notion of chatter as the music of spoken language lies in tension with listeners' desires to grasp what is being said, as Lansky notes:

> The incoherent babble of Idle Chatter is really a pretext to create a complicated piece in which you think you can 'parse the data', but are constantly surprised and confused. The texture is designed to make it seem as if the words, rhythms and harmonies are understandable, but what results, I think, is a musical surface with a lot of places around which your ear can dance while you vainly try to figure out what is going on.[32]

This resonates with what Luciano Berio said of his *Sinfonia* (1968), where 'the experience of "not quite hearing" ... is to be conceived as essential to the nature of the work itself'. For Berio this meant mixing multiple sources – the words of Beckett, Joyce and 'slogans written by the students on the walls of the Sorbonne during the May 1968 insurrection' – to form a sonic palimpsest.[33] The music is analogous to the noisy texts of Joyce's final novels, discussed in the last chapter, with Berio similarly acting as radio receiver to multiple channels. This notion was made more explicit by Karlheinz Stockhausen in 1969 in the notes for a recording of his composition *Hymnen*: 'Out of an international gibberish of short wave broadcasts, its form becomes rigorous and strongly directional.'[34]

International Gibberish

To return to sound poetry, how can we always be sure that what we're hearing is gibberish in languages other than our own? As we've already seen, Bob Cobbing was fond of mixing real words from languages other than English with phoney terms that evoked foreign words. As Jean-Jacques Lecercle says of unfamiliar words, 'One can never be certain that the "coined" word one discovers in a text does not have existence, and conventional meaning, in a larger dictionary or a specialised jargon.'[35] Or, we might add, in another global tongue. Bob Cobbing and François Dufrêne play on the nonsense of foreign tongues in their collaborative piece 'Slowly, Slowly the Tongue Unrolls', which operates as a game of Anglo-French misunderstanding.[36] Even though they descend into gobbledygook, the attempts between the speakers to speak each other's languages initially sound serious enough. This means that, as with Lucier's voice continuing to 'speak' to us even after it has been subsumed into the room's frequencies, the words spoken by Cobbing and Dufrêne still sound like their respective languages. To take an earlier example, Malcolm Green suggests that Hugo Ball's sound poem 'Karawane' 'is "comprehensible" to the German reader in much the same way as Carroll's *Jabberwocky* [to the English reader]'.[37] While this is questionable (because Ball's poem has less regular words and is not presented in the regular garb of language that Carroll's poem is), it's certainly German-flavoured, just as Mimmo Rotella's phonetic poems are Italian-flavoured.[38]

Jaap Blonk often plays with the flavour of different languages in his work. One of his pieces consists of the sounds in Dutch which are particularly challenging for non-native speakers but doesn't actually resort to using proper words. Another way of invoking inter-language confusion is with sound or homophonic translation. Ernst Jandl's 'surface translation' of William Wordsworth's 'My Heart Leaps Up When I Behold' includes the lines 'seht steil dies fader rosse mähen / in teig kurt wisch mai desto bier / baum deutsche deutsch bajonett schulr eiertier' as a translation of 'the child is father of the man / and I could wish my days to be / bound each to each by natural piety'; the 'translation' becomes evident when the 'German' version is read aloud with an ear to hearing English.[39] The 'mother goose' rhymes of Luis van Rooten, cited in Chapter 1, provide further examples of what Etienne Souriau refers to as *baragouin*, the 'playful imitation of a foreign tongue'. This, along with Souriau's other types of imaginary languages – *charabia*, '"regularly" invented words', and *lanternois*, 'proliferation of obsessional phonemes' – are as pertinent to the world of sound poetry as they are to nonsense literature.[40]

Nonsense translation is taken to an extreme by the 'vocal arts and sound poetry' label Atemwerft with its 'Vocology' series. One of their albums is called *Voices of Babel // Babel of Voices* and purports to tell 'the story of the Tower of Babel read in modern constructed languages'; another, *Dada Data Wrecking Ball*, consists of TTS (text-to-speech) engines reading and translating poems by Hugo Ball; titles include 'Seepferdchen und Flugfische' read by Google Translate and converted to Japanese; 'Katzen und Pfauen' read by Bing Translator; and 'Who goes to the Ball, and who is Hugo Ball?' read by the United Voices of Google Translate, conducted by Martyn Schmidt.[41] As well as the nonsense created by the inability of software programmes to read or translate all the words, added sonic play is created by the machine voices, which navigate a confused path between logical authority and vulnerability. In another case of machinic translation, Bernhard Gál's contribution to a project called *Henri Chopin Remixed* plays with the musicality of the voice as it transforms semi-intelligible fragments of the sound poet's speech into robotic mutations. For much of the piece there is a 'Frenchness' to the vocal sounds, even when precise words cannot be determined. The robotically pitched voices, meanwhile, resonate with the use of similar metallic tones used in science fiction. The dialectic of techno-authority and techno-vulnerability is a common one in film, television, radio and music, where machinic failure is connected to lapses in logical sense, often leading to robotic nonsense.[42]

Cutting and Plundering

In 1958, John Cage composed a vocal piece of indeterminate length after being inspired by the singing of Cathy Berberian, Berio's wife and artistic collaborator. 'Aria' uses a range of vocal sounds – including words from Armenian, Russian, Italian, French and English – and cuts between them in a manner that corresponds to Cage's 'Williams Mix' (1958), a piece with which it was sometimes combined. While both works anticipated future developments in cut-up audio, plunderphonics and sampling, there are important differences between the two. Not the least is that 'Williams Mix' was a finished piece created by cutting and splicing tape recordings of instrumental and electronic sounds, while 'Aria' was an open score to be performed live using the human voice. This gives the latter piece a distinct resonance with sound poetry, and with the melding of words, music and 'international gibberish' that Stockhausen and Berio were exploring. What these Cage pieces have in common is a fascination with the chance procedures enabled by the recomposition of existing sources. This was a theme dear to Joyce, as noted in the previous chapter, and to many other modernists: Hannah Höch's collages and Tristan Tzara's cut-up newspaper poems were part of the Dada artistic fabric; Russolo's art of noises expressed a desire to sample the various sounds of industry and technological progress; Dziga Vertov's Laboratory of Hearing brought sonic montage to Russian Futurism; T.S. Eliot and Ezra Pound raided the past for the benefit of present innovations. The result was what James Rother refers to as '"moog" eclecticism', a synthesizing process suited to the century of recorded sound.[43]

Crucial to the notion of synthesis as it developed in the twentieth century was the idea of reconfiguring fragments into multiple permutations. In the world of poetry, this is exemplified by the permutation poems of Brion Gysin, which typically take a four- or five-word phrase and gradually rearrange the order of the words until all permutations have been exhausted. The poems exist on paper and as computer programs, but of main relevance to this book is what happens when the poems are read aloud. There are numerous recordings available of Gysin reading the poems, though it is also rewarding for any reader to recite them, as different patterns will emerge with each interpreter. Indeed, the poems invite recitation rather than silent reading; where the eye quickly gets the point, parses the 'gimmick' and is ready to move, the mouth is forced to linger on the challenges and pleasures of the permutated words, savouring the new sounds produced by the recombined and looped texts. Reading the permutation poem 'I Don't Work You Dig', for example, a reader might make associations with jazz and pop music due in part to the way that the word 'dig' has been used by musicians, critics and fans, and also due to the way that the word dances around the line, popping up in different places in each of the poem's thirty lines ('work dig I don't you / you work dig I don't / dig I don't you work', etc.).[44] The words 'man habit' that crop up in one of the lines to 'Kick That Habit Man' can sound like 'inhabit', though the words on the page would not suggest this.

Gysin's own recordings often create different meanings to those suggested by a neutral recitation of the shifting words. To my ear they possess less open-endedness than might be expected, instead showing how the poem as score can lend itself to emotive expression (which, presumably, was Gysin's intent, even if I have been led to read the poems differently in my own vocalization). Gysin tends to stress certain words at the expense of others, making each line a statement in its own right rather than letting each flow into the next. The result is that each line sounds deliberately composed rather than automatically generated. This is emphasized further in a recorded collaboration with saxophonist Steve Lacy in which three of the permutation poems (including 'I Don't Work You Dig') are set to musical accompaniment. There are noticeable culminations at the end of each line or word group, made more obvious by brief pauses between each line, as well as emotional emphasis on certain words and phrases. Gysin also made a recording of the poem 'I Am That I Am' in which he adds technical manipulation via tape dubbing, adding emphasis both at the level of the phrase (so that each occurrence of 'Am I' becomes a question: sometimes '*am* I?', sometimes 'am *I*?') and at the technological level as echo, reverb and tape speed add new blocks of sense. Gysin's description of this recording as a 'machine-poem' suggests that the machinic in language (working parts, movement, repetition) mixes with the machinic sound reproduction technology.[45]

Bob Cobbing also used the permutation technique; his poem 'Make perhaps this out sense of can you', which opens the posthumous collection *Boooook*, consists of permutations of the phrase 'Perhaps you can make sense out of this'.[46] For Cobbing, the visual look of poems was as important as the sound and, as with so many of the small press pamphlets and chap-books published during his long career, *Boooook* is as much a work of visual art as of literature. It is also a score, a reminder that many of Cobbing's sound poems began life as concrete poems and vice versa. The poem 'oslo solo', for example, is both an elegant piece of typesetting, in which the four letters of these words are placed in different combinations like a word game (so so, sol. los, o, lo, etc.) and an invitation to try out the shifting sonic patterns created by phonemic mixing.[47] The process can be observed in a collection of poems edited by Cobbing and Bill Griffiths entitled *Verbi Visi Voco*, whose name comes from a line in *Finnegans Wake* in which Joyce writes of a 'verbivocovisual presentment of the world'; work is included by Hugo Ball, John Cage, Allen Ginsberg, Cobbing, bpNichol and Steve McCaffery.[48]

The cut-up techniques explored by Brion Gysin and William Burroughs provide another way of thinking about a 'verbivocovisual presentment of the world'. Like Gysin's permutation poems, cut-ups are generally about rearranging syntax to rearrange semantics and lead to new discoveries. Where permutation aimed for a liberation of semantics through rhythm, cut-ups were more obviously aligned to collages, montages and mixes, where new relationships could be formed through juxtaposition. While often written about as textual strategies (the visual artist's collage brought to the writer), cut-ups produced by Gysin, Burroughs and John Giorno in the 1960s were also sound experiments, using the tape recorder to break free of what Burroughs saw as the control system of everyday language. Even when working only with written texts, however, Burroughs and Gysin saw the results of cut-ups in terms of sound as much as vision. In an observation that shares some of the insights proposed in Mikhail Bakhtin's work on the dialogical aspect of written texts, Burroughs claimed 'all writing is in fact cut-ups. A collage of words read heard overheard. What else? The use of scissors renders the process explicit and subject to extension and variation. ... Images shift sense under the scissors smell images to sound sight to sound sound to kinaesthetic.'[49] There was a shamanistic aspect to the practice too; by cutting up Shakespeare or Rimbaud, Burroughs argued, their voices could be heard as if in the same room.[50]

The cut-up techniques utilized by Gysin and Burroughs would go on to influence several popular musicians, including David Bowie, Iggy Pop, Patti Smith, Cabaret Voltaire and Kurt Cobain, while Gysin's permutation poems have also been cited as models for the work of Philip Glass and Daevid Allen.[51] For lyricists, text cut-ups operated as devices for writing songs, while sonic cut-ups suggested ways in which composers and remixers could rearrange sonic reality. In the Czechoslovakia of the 1960s, Milan Knížák put on ritualistic happenings in the streets of Prague before moving to sound-based work that included the physical alteration and mutilation of vinyl records. Works such as *Broken Music* applied cut-up techniques to records, cracking, dismantling and rebuilding them so that they played reconfigured music. Later, in New York, Christian Marclay worked with broken and cut-up records on projects which complemented his work in the visual arts, while Yasunao Tone performed similar mutilations on compact discs, 'wounding' them to change and distort their data. German band Oval was instrumental in turning the sound of CD malfunction into aesthetically pleasing music, using glitch as a texture in pop songs.[52]

Marclay's work allows us to think of questions at least tangential, if not always central, to this book's themes, in particular the narrative of the vinyl record. As a technology, records have a prescribed use that follows the narrative logic of the needle in the groove. Marclay and other artists who work with records interrupt this narrative logic and create new narratives of their own, as in Knížák's and Marclay's broken and rebuilt records. Another technique is the speeding up and slowing down of records via the tools of the turntable. On *More Encores* (1989), Marclay works with the narrative logics not only of the record but of the musical genres with which he's engaging. Each track is named after the musician whose records he is manipulating. In 'Johann Strauss' he manipulates the record right at the point where Strauss's dance music is emphasizing the beat (lurching towards it as dancers would lurch towards it), making it even more exaggerated and causing a destabilizing quality that is inimical to actual dancing. Rather than the music leading the dance, the reverse happens as Marclay effectively dances with the record. With 'John Zorn' he exaggerates the fractured nature of Zorn's playing, forcing his records to emit jagged fragments of sound, while 'Martin Denny' is exotica gone dark and brooding. For 'Louis Armstrong' Marclay uses a hand-cranked gramophone both as a conceptual nod to authenticity but also as a way of getting yet more bodily involvement with the technology through the particular mechanics of the player. On 'Maria Callas' we hear fetishized moments of pure voice, where the opera voice becomes more about music and sound than about sense. This is an extended example of what Michel Poizat calls the transformation of the diva into 'pure voice', with language transformed into obsessively repeated sound and endlessly deferred meaning.[53] Much of this is non-vocal instrumental music to begin with and it all becomes instrumental in its recomposition. We can't necessarily extrapolate from this a general theory of sense and meaning in non-vocal or non-verbal music, but we can at least point to questions that are worth asking even as they exceed the parameters of this study: Can instrumental music be said to 'make sense' and, if so, to make 'nonsense'?

A related example is the work *Lost Objects*, with a libretto by Deborah Artman and music by Michael Gordon, David Lang and Julia Wolfe, performed by Bang on a Can, Concerto Köln, RIAS-Kammerchor and remixed by DJ Spooky. The connecting theme throughout is loss, whether related to objects, people, languages or musical sounds. 'Not Our Darkness (Loss of Meaning)' deals directly with semantics and represents the point where, as Artman says, 'language disintegrates into babble'. This is represented in the libretto through the gradual abbreviation of the phrase 'It's not our darkness that we fear ... but our light' to 'our darkness we fear / light', and finally just 'fear / light'. Reflecting on the various ways in which *Lost Objects* engages with sonic loss, Artman suggests that having DJ Spooky remix some of the music creates 'transformations, variations, alterations of our already lost sound'.[54] The 'already lost' sound she refers to is the result of a creative decision to have the instruments tuned to 'baroque pitch', but I'd suggest that a libretto sung by a classical or operatic singer is also a kind of lost sound. This may seem an odd thing to say given the general acceptance of such vocal styles as representative of Western culture, but I would argue that the classical or operatic voice, while still perhaps retaining its cultural capital as the representative of a classical ideal in singing, in fact obscures as much as it communicates (hence Poizat's 'pure voice').

As a way of considering both the remixed sound text and the extent to which samples of pre-existing recordings can be made sense of when placed at the service of new narratives, it is instructive to listen to the plunderphonic work of John Oswald. Oswald sees himself working in a lineage that includes Burroughs and Gysin and has also produced a plunderphonic mix of Burroughs's speaking voice which uses sonic palindromes and repeated phonemes to make Burroughs's words (more) nonsensical.[55] He is better known, however, for his reworkings of popular music and his aim has generally been to use the smallest fragments of the recordings that would still allow the source to be recognized; this irreducible slice of the pop text is what he defines as the 'plunderphone'.[56] Oswald is also interested in the visual and textual accompaniments to his recordings and so he attributes his pieces to remixed names, such as Bing Stingspreen, Ice Garfunkle, Halen Oates, Marianne Faith No Morrissey, 10,000 Megasmiths, Julian Lennox and Public Enya. Record and CD sleeves likewise come adorned with visually remixed versions of iconic pop star images.

As with other nonsense strategies, something original remains for the listening ear to make sense of even while trying to make sense of the new text being audited. The latter could be heard as a musical sense-making and the former as a more verbal one, except that the sources Oswald plunders are often already musical texts, meaning that the verbal communication was already a musical one as well. Rather, perhaps what we need to distinguish is a type of sense-making that exists at the level of the phrase, whether verbal or not, and another at the level of the unit (the phoneme, museme or plunderphone), with the latter being closer to the Barthesian 'grain' that communicates to us in the voices we derive pleasure from. The difference here would be that Oswald presents us with a constantly changing grain, which becomes not only the main attraction, but also the main distraction as the listener scoops reference points from the tunes hurtling by. Reflecting on Oswald's plunderphonic piece *Plexure* (built from thousands of sampled records released between 1982 and 1992), Carl Wilson suggests that 'with all it has to say about pop music, remembrances of things past, aural doppelgangers, surfaces and essences ... perhaps the greatest challenge of *Plexure* is to listen to it as music rather than as commentary, as self-contained content rather than a palimpsest of infinite contexts'.[57]

At the same time, there is arguably as much 'sense' in the new text as there was in the old, perhaps more. An element that might have gone relatively unnoticed in its original context becomes fetishized when singled out for attention, coming to seem more important due to its treatment. This happens with *Grayfolded*, Oswald's epic reworking of the Grateful Dead song 'Dark Star'. Unlike the pieces made up of thousands of different songs, *Grayfolded* combines fragments of multiple live recordings of the same song, stretching it out into a vast multi-tracked megaversion. As laid out in a soundmap of the piece provided in the CD booklet, *Grayfolded* is structured around lyrical fragments. 'Dark Star' has minimal lyrics and mainly functioned as a framework for extended jams by the Grateful Dead, so there was already a logic of extension even before Oswald performed his song-stretching. Referring to one of the lyrical fragments, the band's songwriter Robert Hunter says, 'I don't have any idea what "the transitive nightfall of diamonds" means. It sounded good at the time.'[58] That 'meaninglessness' in the original is then exaggerated by Oswald in his manipulation of the Dead 'choir' that appears in *Grayfolded*.

Techniques of slurring, time-stretching, pitch-shifting and related sonic treatments can be traced through the history of popular music from dub to hip-hop, techno and electronic dance music. As the fracturing of verbal and musical texts into nonsensical fragments became normalized in popular music practice, so sonic texts would be versioned and reversioned in a continual dialogical practice that often reconfigured basic building blocks of meaning, such as phonemes, syllables, morphemes, words, musemes, riffs and other rhythmic and semiotic units.[59] Take, for example, Fatboy Slim's 1998 remix of Wildchild's 'Renegade Master', a reworking that performs a severe breakdown of the semantic content of its source material. The track's prehistory can be traced to 1979, when rapper Spoonie Gee released 'Spoonin' Rap'. A line from that track ('One for the trouble, two for the time') was sampled for A.D.O.R.'s 1994 hip-hop track 'One for the Trouble'. This track in turn was sampled and provided the title for the 1995 club track by Wildchild but without the Spoonie Gee sample; now the lines being singled out were 'back once again for the renegade master', 'D for damager', 'power to the people' and 'with the ill behaviour', which are chopped and spliced elements from A.D.O.R.'s lines (two of which are 'back once again with the ill behaviour, can you feel it?' and 'It's the A for ally, D for damager'). For the 1998 remix, Fatboy Slim added further loops and permutations that break the lyrics down to words, parts of words, phonemes and even sub-phonemic vocal atoms, the latter spliced together so closely as to resemble vibration rather than speech (not unlike what happens in Henri Chopin's 'Rouge'). Towards the end, the line 'with the ill behaviour' is looped into a rapid repeat which then gradually blurs and slurs, the phonics briefly becoming something like the mutated voice of Lucier's *I Am Sitting in a Room*.[60]

As always, the extent to which the track is nonsensical depends on the context. Whereas the raps by Spoonie Gee and A.D.O.R. are clearly meant to be heard as narratives, with the stories becoming a main aspect of the meaning of the track, the tracks by Wildchild and Fatboy Slim use vocal fragments purely as rhythmic elements with a minimal semantic value. It is not so much a difference between narrative vocals and dance music (Spoonie Gee's track is party hip-hop, after all, and quite conducive to dancing), but the imagined state of mind of those listening; in much the same way that Hugo Ball saw nonsensical sound poems as a way of inducing a Dada state of mind, so the 1990s dance tracks are classic examples of club 'bangers' aimed at altered states of consciousness; one only has to read the comments sections under online postings of 'Renegade Master' for evidence of how the track (and its remixed versions) has remained in the memory of clubbers of the time. If 'Renegade Master' made, and still makes, perfect sense when placed in context, is it wrong to single it out as an example of sonic nonsense making? It can easily be argued that that this is just one way of making affective functional music. Thinking about it this way, the track does not really comment on its predecessors (especially Spoonie Gee, whose words no longer feature in the sonic mix), but is rather an entirely new text. Even so, by placing these four tracks together, we are alerted to the very deliberate manipulations of electronic music producers who recognize the affective power of words in sonic texts. Words are not essential to electronic dance music after all, as countless vocal-less tracks show. They are clearly not an accidental presence in 'Renegade Master' but rather a way into the track, a link that connects words and song and rhythm and dancing. Their presence operates as a mnemonic device; I, for one, find it easier to remember how 'Renegade Master' goes if I think of the 'lyrics', and I have progressively more difficulty remembering, and certainly vocalizing, the track as these lyrics break down into phonemic units. This contrasts with the experience I have with some other songs, where I can remember the tune more easily than the specific lyrics or their relative order.

Sampling and looping became prominent tools for pop in the late twentieth century and into the twenty-first. Sometimes this work has intersected with the worlds of sound poetry and experimental sonic art referred to in this chapter;[61] more often, it has continued as a vernacular process independent of that longer history, with samplers and remixers finding historical precedents in the dialogic practices of everyday culture. At times, the worlds meet, as with artists like Oswald, Marclay, People Like Us, the Avalanches and Den Sorte Skole, leading to a mix of registers which expand nonsense's sonic palette.[62] In recent years the growth of social media and online sharing cultures has led to a situation whereby cutting, plundering and mashing-up are ubiquitous practices, while the viral nature of meme culture means that the sounds of the past are forever finding new uses. The social life of nonsense requires the recycling of sonic pasts in ever new and surprising ways.

4

Pop Hearts Nonsense

The Music of the Word

John Giorno suggests that something was lost, or perhaps transposed, when would-be poets turned to music instead of 'die-hard' poetry. 'I have a theory', he says, 'that from the '50s on, countless kids who were poets by nature were given electric guitars for Christmas. They fiddled around with the chords, and words arose in their minds – they experimented with words and music and the great ones became rock stars. It's only die-hard poets, like me, who stayed true to the music inherent in the word.'[1] In making this point, Giorno is tapping into a fairly common observation that popular music took over from poetry as a form of romantic youthful expression. Having worked with rock bands himself, Giorno is keen to point out that the distinction he makes is really one that hinges on the naturalness of performance, which seems to come more easily for most rock stars than for most poets. But there is also, in his claim, a seeming distinction between the poem as written and the poem or song as performed, a distinction made more explicitly by other poets who have considered the relationship between the oral and the written word. Jacques Roubaud, in a short text about poetry and orality that serves as a prelude to *The Sound of Poetry / The Poetry of Sound*, argues that sound poetry and popular music should be thought of as types of spectacle or performance rather than poetry, which, for him, requires a continuing relationship to the written word: 'If one were to commit to paper what normally constitutes this type of "poetry" – assuming it contains words from any given language – we would be in the presence of an absolutely mediocre text.'[2]

It is no doubt such lingering doubts about the place of popular song as poetry that caused consternation in some quarters when, in 2016, it was announced that Bob Dylan was to be awarded the Nobel Prize in Literature 'for having created new poetic expressions within the great American song tradition'. For traditionalists (that is, those whose idea of tradition did not extend as far back as Homer), the granting of such a prestigious literary prize to a singer-songwriter was an insult to a host of deserving international writers who had devoted their lives to the supposed 'higher arts' of text-based poetry and prose. For others, including members of the Swedish Academy, Dylan's words worked as well on the page as on the record; 'He can be read and should be read, and is a great poet in the English tradition,' argued Sara Danius, permanent secretary of the academy.[3] Reflecting on this, I wonder whether there is an imbalance between the claims made for literature's ability (and occasional need) to tap into primeval sound/music (made evident in the claims of the Dadaists, Futurists, sound poets and many more besides) and those made for music's ability (and occasional need) to be literate.

There is certainly no dearth of pop artists who have deliberately set out to explore the music of words as explicitly as, and for similar reasons to, many of the artists already discussed. The extent to which this is theorized outside of the music, as it were, varies depending largely on the 'art worlds' that musicians, critics and fans see themselves as operating within (or across).[4] In this chapter, I first consider musicians working within popular music who have either made explicit connections to artistic practices discussed earlier in the book or whose work has been connected through critical exegesis. Following this, I turn to some of the many examples in which popular song engages with the sound of nonsense, regardless of whether the artists in question intended such connections to be made. In such cases, the sound of nonsense relies on connections made through 'the ear of the behearer'.[5]

As much as I believe in popular music's ability to reflect and inform the most serious aspects of our lives, I also revel in pop's love affair with nonsense. I hear nonsense as one of the sources of pop's vitality, with vitality signifying both dynamism and importance. Nonsense sounds, as exuberant outpourings, are part of the very life force of songs and singing and, while by no means obligatory, have long been part of the common vocabulary of much popular song. This was something which the Beatles understood very well and which enabled them to retain a lightness of tone in their work even as they were partly responsible for the growing recognition of popular music as serious art in the 1960s. The group combined the nonsense traditions inherent in doo-wop and rock 'n' roll with a cultural inheritance that included the Goons and Ivor Cutler (who appeared in their film *Magical Mystery Tour*), leading to a particularly British nonsensicality. Songs as different as 'Ob-La-Di, Ob-La-Da' and 'I Am the Walrus' showcased a mix of humour, psychedelia, surrealism and whimsy indebted to music hall and nonsense traditions, while John Lennon's books *In His Own Write* (1964) and *A Spaniard in the Works* (1965) paid homage to precursors from Lear and Carroll to Spike Milligan. It is interesting to note that the decade that the Beatles helped define was one in which popular culture aligned itself with a range of spiritual, cultural and psychic quests, notable in the searching jazz of John Coltrane, the Beatles' collaboration with Ravi Shankar, the Coltrane- and Shankar-inspired 'raga rock' of the Byrds, and the general emphasis on psychedelic music and consciousness-altering drugs. Many cultural artefacts of the time connected such quests to the nonsense tradition, obvious examples being Jonathan Miller's trippy film adaptation of *Alice in Wonderland*, with its Shankar soundtrack, and Jefferson Airplane's Alice-referencing 'White Rabbit', intended by its composer Grace Slick as a comment on parental hypocrisy but heard generally as an endorsement of the acid experience.

Another 1960s group who combined an interest in classic nonsense, Dada, surrealism and a strand of British humour running back at least as far as the Victorian music hall was the Bonzo Dog Doo-Dah Band. The group consisted of art students who originally viewed it as a project tangential to their studies and whose particular brand of Dada included scouring antique shops and markets for old records – particularly 78s of the interwar period – and mining them for their comic potential. The group's name was also an act of repurposing, inspired by the Bonzo the Dog character that appeared on postcards from the 1920s. Recordings by the Bonzos mixed nonsensical narratives, musical parodies and silly noises, with musical references that took in 1930s novelty foxtrots, blues, rock and psychedelia.[6] In some ways they were the flipside to the increasing seriousness being attached to popular music from the mid-1960s onwards; while the group were friends with the Beatles and shared a similar taste for whimsy and the absurd, it's possible that the Bonzos were too silly even for the nonsense-loving Fab Four. Some of their finest moments were also flipsides, such as the B-side to their one and only hit, 'I'm the Urban Spaceman'. Where the Neil Innes-penned A-side featured a catchy pop song that could have sprung from any number of beat groups of the time, the B-side delivered a more typical mix of parody, surrealism and sonic silliness in the form of Vivian Stanshall's 'Canyons of Your Mind'. In a mock-sincere spoken welcome, Stanshall begins with 'This is the B-side of our platter, sports fans, and I'm singing just for you covered in sequins', before starting to sing in a deep Elvis-like voice. The lyrics are overwrought and bathetic, but also weirdly detailed: 'In the canyons of your mind / I will wander through your brain / To the ventricles of your heart, my dear.' As the song progresses the lyrics become stranger until, following a mangled guitar solo, the singer evokes the 'cardboard-coloured dreams' in which he kisses his darling's 'perfumed hair / the sweet essence of giraffe'. The group also challenges the notion of innocuous backing vocals by having the musicians sing words that have nothing to do with the main lyric; counterpoised against the line 'Every time I hear your name' is the line 'frying pan, frying pan'. 'Canyons of Your Mind' was the reverse side of everyday rationality, a topsy-turvy, carnivalesque riposte to straight society.[7]

Like Lewis Carroll and Edward Lear, the Bonzos highlighted the thin line between nonsense and parody; sometimes, a nonsense strategy will result in parody and sometimes a parodic strategy can result in nonsense. In the spoken finale to 'My Pink Half of the Drainpipe', Stanshall intones a nonsense strategy to be used against a dull neighbour: 'Norman, if you're normal, I intend to be a freak for the rest of my life, and I shall baffle you with cabbages and rhinoceroses in the kitchen, incessant quotations from "Now We Are Six" through the mouthpiece of Lord Snooty's giant poisoned electric head.'[8] Like the B-side of the platter, the pink half of the drainpipe was an opportunity to impose nonsense strategies on 'innocent' others, strategies which Stanshall pursued in his career outside the Doo-Dah Band. His single 'Labio Dental Fricative' contained nonsense lines based on tongue-twisting alliteration ('Cannibal chiefs chew Camembert cheese / cause chewing keeps 'em cheeky' and 'How many pies can a porpoise poise on purpose if she pleases'), contradiction ('I got up at eight, it was half past two') and plain silliness ('He took off his hat, and he took off his head / took off Max Bygraves, here's what he said').⁹ He also created the character Sir Henry at Rawlinson End for a series of broadcasts which appeared irregularly on John Peel's BBC Radio programme. Peel's show was a natural home for Stanshall's brand of nonsense, where it sat alongside other Peel favourites such as Ivor Cutler and Robert Wyatt, artists working at the interface of art and popular music and doing so with a love of the nonsense tradition, whether voiced in the English whimsy of Stanshall and Wyatt or the melancholy 'Scotch' magical realism of Cutler.¹⁰ Peel's show, as the go-to site for 'alternative' music on national radio, acted as a B-side to daytime pop culture even as the two facets remained irremovably conjoined. Like Wyatt and Cutler, Stanshall explored the possibilities of sound to deliver nonsensical narratives. In his case, he framed his absurdities with the kind of 'no-nonsense' voice that can be detected in Carroll's prose and which is made manifest in so many audiobook versions of the Alice stories. In Stephen Fry's evocative description, 'it's a very odd voice inasmuch as the typical Vivian Stanshall song can be a very light, almost '20s crooning voice ... or it can be an extremely rich, incredibly English [voice]. It reeks of Mullard valves covered in dust from old wireless sets and a sort of South Coast, vaguely colonial sense to it.'¹¹

Dada Funk

Other artists working in the popular music sphere have also made explicit reference to the sound artists of the past. These include Brian Eno, who sampled Kurt Schwitters's *Ursonate* on his 1977 song 'Kurt's Rejoinder', and Talking Heads, who adapted a Hugo Ball sound poem as the opening track of their 1979 album *Fear of Music*. Jonathan Lethem describes 'I Zimbra' – the title Talking Heads used for Ball's 'Gadji Beri Bimba' – as an example of Morse code introducing *Fear of Music*, a transmission of something which the listener can't (yet) understand but in which she can recognize a meaning to mean. Lethem provides a transcription of how an English speaker might understand the words by transliterating them ('Gadget berry bomber clamored'), using what he calls 'the fool's yearning spell-check of the ear'.¹² Referring to Ball's 'drillsargeanty nonsense', Lethem notes that 'a song or poem composed in an invented language foregrounds the labor of memorization that's normally taken for granted in performance'. This practice can be related to the memory feats undertaken by Jaap Blonk and other *Ursonate* performers, the 'logatomes' identified by Hermann Ebbinghaus in his memory experiments, and the 'acoustic-iconic mnemonic systems' studied by the ethnomusicologist David Hughes.[13]

Other pop references to the Dada era include the band Cabaret Voltaire and the label ZTT (named after Marinetti's 'Zang Tumb Tumb'), home to Frankie Goes to Hollywood, Propaganda, cut-up experimenters Art of Noise (named after the work by Marinetti's fellow Futurist Luigi Russolo) and 808 State. In 2010, the nonsensically named Chumbawamba released 'Ratatatay', a song based on an oft-repeated tale about George Melly using Schwitters's *Ursonate* to deter would-be muggers. The verses tell the story in standard language and are interspersed with the only slightly nonsensical refrain that gives the song its title. Later in the song, some of the sounds of the *Ursonate* are incorporated and run into the refrain, sonically melding Schwitters's sound with those more likely to be heard in the folk music that was influencing Chumbawamba at this point in the band's career.[14]

Bobs

Nonsense strategies as ways of policing insider and outsider knowledge can be found repeatedly in the work of Bob Dylan, not only his extensive songwriting across multiple musical styles, but also his infamous interactions with critics, fans and interviewers. At the height of his fame and notoriety in the 1960s, Dylan turned such encounters into staged confrontations that divided actors into those who got what he was doing and those who did not, with Dylan deploying tactics that wouldn't have been out of place among Dadaists, absurdists or surrealists.[15] Dylan frequently drew on this tension as a source of inspiration for his songwriting, for example in the searing critique that drives his 1965 song 'Ballad of a Thin Man'. The song relates the predicament of an artist faced with countless intrusions on his time and privacy and the arguably greater predicament of Mr Jones, the hapless square who stumbles into the artist's hipster world and is then critiqued mercilessly. In its presentation of tensions that arise from conflicting understandings of an event or scene, 'Ballad of a Thin Man' is somewhat like the Alice stories, in which, as Marnie Parsons writes, 'the uncontainable forces of change and contradiction, the variations and vanishing in Wonderland leave even Alice's, that most stubborn and staid of minds, reeling'.[16] This applies just as well to Dylan's hapless Mr Jones, whose mind is left reeling by the contradictions, variations and vanishings he encounters. But where Parsons uses the word 'even', we might argue that it's precisely *because* these minds are stubborn and staid that they are left reeling. While we could expect a defiant stubbornness to continue unaffected regardless of what is sent to challenge it, we must also recognize that the stubbornness – the squareness – is part of the reason that insufficiently flexible minds get blown. The bluffness of the no-nonsense attitude is defused by nonsense; Alice and Mr Jones may not get it, but they can't come away unaffected.

One of the most effective nonsense strategies used in Dylan's song is the nonsense conversation, a dialogue which seems to be following normal rules of turn-taking but which finds the parties unable to connect. This is a technique found in many of the plays of Samuel Beckett; when we witness Mr Jones having to deal with exchanges such as '"Is this where it is?" ... "It's his" ... "What's mine?" ... "Where what is?"' or '"NOW" ... "For what reason?" ... "How?" ... "What does this mean?" ... "You're a cow, give me some milk or else go home"', we may well be put in mind of the riddling conversational duels fought by Estragon and Vladimir in *Waiting for Godot*, Hamm and Clov in *Endgame*, or Willie and Winnie in *Happy Days*.[17] Such nonsense strategies can be found throughout Dylan's work, whether he is drawing on the timeless nonsense of American vernacular music – in a process that aligns his songwriting with many of the other musicians discussed in this chapter – or on characters, plots and approaches derived from literature, theatre and the visual arts. Reflecting on Dylan's 1966 album *Blonde on Blonde*, the journalist Ed Vulliamy writes, 'the ironically charged meaning of nonsense, and the nonsense in everything; I heard it first across those four sides of vinyl'.[18] Like classic nonsense writers, Dylan's riddling work has generated endless speculation over meaning. When he sings lines such as 'the sun's not yellow, it's chicken', 'he went off sniffing drainpipes and reciting the alphabet', 'he just smoked my eyelids, and punched my cigarette' or 'I walked by a Guernsey cow, who directed me down to the Bowery slums', this is riddling nonsense of the kind Jean-Jacques Lecercle discusses; we want to make sense of these proclamations because, like classic riddles, they *'must* have a solution'.[19] In the exegesis of work by Lewis Carroll and Bob Dylan – and both writers have inspired small libraries of such work – what they say must make sense because they are seen, heard and read as visionaries.

I also find Dylan's songs very Joycean and, specifically, *Finneganswakean*. There's a sense of all time being present and a huge array of historical actors sharing space in the story; in 'Desolation Row' alone, we encounter Cinderella, Bette Davis, Romeo, Cain and Abel, the Hunchback of Notre Dame, the Good Samaritan, Ophelia, Noah, Nero, 'Einstein disguised as Robin Hood', Dr Filth, the Phantom of the Opera, Casanova, Ezra Pound, T. S. Eliot, and other anonymous figures such as 'the blind commissioner', 'the fortune-telling lady', 'a jealous monk' and some calypso singers. Such an assemblage resonates with a description of *Finnegans Wake* by Joseph Campbell and Henry Morton Robinson:

> On this revolving stage, mythological heroes and events of remotest antiquity occupy the same spatial and temporal planes as modern personages and contemporary happenings. All time occurs simultaneously; Tristram and the Duke of Wellington, Father Adam and Humpty Dumpty merge in a single percept.[20]

And with this from Terence McKenna:

> *Finnegans Wake* is as if you had taken the entirety of the last thousand years of human history and dissolved all the boundaries, so Queen Mab becomes Mae West [and] all the personages of pop culture, politics, art, church history, Irish legend, Irish internecine politics, are all swirling, changing, merging. Time is not linear. You will find yourself at a recent political rally, then return to the court of this or that Abyssinian emperor or pharaoh. It's like a trip.[21]

Both passages seem apt for many of Dylan's songs, from the historically surreal to those that are saturated in folk history. The journeys described in songs such as 'On the Road Again' and 'Bob

Dylan's 115th Dream' are journeys into the imagination, trippy in both the drug-related sense that McKenna is alluding to and in terms of the surreal world of dreams and nightmares. There is also an engagement with childlike logic; in 'I Shall Be Free No. 10', from *Another Side Of*, Dylan mixes number and letter games with dreamlike imagery, suggesting a surreal take on the children's songs recorded by one of his early influences, Woody Guthrie.

As well as drawing on a long tradition of vernacular music, Dylan has inspired countless subsequent artists, many of whom have shown their debt through cover versions of his songs. There are also Dylan parodies, which build further layers of sense-making (and sense-befuddling) on already nonsensical texts. 'Weird Al' Yankovic's 'Bob' is a prime example, a style parody that responds to Dylan's sound (particularly his mid-1960s sound) and to the befuddling nature of some of his lyrics. One of the specific songs it parodies is 'Subterranean Homesick Blues', a reference made most explicitly in the video that accompanies 'Bob'. At the start of D. A. Pennebaker's documentary *Dont Look Back*, Dylan is seen holding up cards with partial lyrics to 'Subterranean Homesick Blues' while the film plays on the soundtrack. Yankovic recreates this footage for his song, substituting Dylan's lyrics for his own, though the musical style of 'Bob' is closer to Dylan's 'Tombstone Blues'. Yankovic plays on the famous inscrutability of Dylan's 1960s lyrics by composing his parody entirely from palindromes such as 'I, man, am Regal, a German am I', 'Madam, I'm Adam', 'Lisa Bonet ate no basil', 'Do geese see God?', 'Do nine men Interpret? Nine men I nod', 'May a moody baby doom a yam', 'O Geronimo, no minor ego', 'Oozy rat in a sanitary zoo' and 'Go hang a salami, I'm a lasagna hog'; the title, too, is a palindrome.[22] Yankovic's vocal timbre, attack, phrasing and rhythm make the song convincingly Dylanesque, while the rhyming palindromes provide a structuring logic to the song and provide it with its own sense even as it makes no sense semantically.

A related approach can be found in Robert Wyatt's 'Blues in Bob Minor', which again is a general stylistic parody/homage rather than being based on any particular song. Like 'Bob', there is specific reference to 'Subterranean Homesick Blues' ('Toe's in the water but you've only got ten', 'Don't take a weathergirl to see where the wind is blowing') and, like Yankovic, Wyatt provides his own lyrics, in this case a relentless stream of word associations.

As Wyatt sings lines such as 'Tunnelling a wormhole Eartha Kitty catfish' and 'Hibernate in winter of our discotheque no end in sight', the words and phrases combine to suggest others: whole earth, Kit Kat, winter of our discontent, techno, insight, and so on.[23] Marnie Parsons's reading of Louis Zukofsky's poem 'Privet' provides a useful comparison; the poem, like Wyatt's, consists of juxtaposed words which are 'seemingly incongruous' but which send out 'sonal shoots' that 'anticipate words that aren't there'.[24] Wyatt's song has an additional effect; in addition to its own internal soundplay, it makes 'sonal' reference to the work of Bob Dylan and therefore acts as a critical reading of Dylan's own linguistic and sonic experimentation.

'Blues in Bob Minor' also fits well into the context of *Shleep* – the album on which it appears – and of Wyatt's work more generally. *Shleep* makes frequent use of dreamlike and childlike narratives; another song on the album bears the Carrollian title 'The Duchess' and uses nursery rhyme and musical nonsense with lines such as 'My wife is sour and sweet / She dit dit dit delete / She's lalala ladida, butter / Secret's safe with me'. Like Bob Cobbing and bpNichol[25] – artists who combined sound poetry, concrete poetry and drawing – Wyatt often has fun with the relationship between written and spoken/sung words. Only from consulting the lyric sheet to *Shleep* do we know that he has written 'butter secret's safe with me'; what we think we hear, of course, is 'but her secret's safe with me'. The lyric sheet also contains drawings by Wyatt and his wife Alfreda Benge (aka Alfie, Alife, Alifib and The Duchess), including a Learesque / Peakesque / Milliganesque / Lennonesque cartoon by Wyatt. A monarch is seated on her throne amidst the clouds, atop a shower of water; the caption reads, 'Queen Victoria rained over her empire for decades'.

More generally, Wyatt's music is marked by a fascination with nonsense verse, wordplay and the construction and deconstruction of linguistic elements. This tendency goes back to his early days with the jazz-rock group Soft Machine (named after a Burroughs novel), whose second album included the two-part 'A Concise British Alphabet' (which involved Wyatt singing the alphabet forwards and backwards), and 'Dada Was Here', on which Wyatt sang and scatted in Spanish. His solo albums have been populated by a range of songs that utilize wordplay or nonsense elements, such as 'The Verb', 'When Access Was a Noun', 'The Duchess' and

'Twas Brillig'. Wyatt has described his work as 'basically out-of-tune nursery rhymes', and it is useful to consider how such rhymes provide us with an early understanding of the relationships between words, rhythms and the musicality of speech.[26] His song 'Alifib/Alife' contains phrases such as 'folly bololey', which could have come straight from Joyce or traditional song, and 'no nit not', which exhibits the monosyllabic pleasure in sound evident in many of Beckett's plays. *Rock Bottom*, the album containing 'Alifib/Alife', also contains the connected pieces 'Little Red Riding Hood Hit the Road' and 'Little Red Robin Hood Hit the Road', which feature the nonsense poet Ivor Cutler.[27] In 1976, Wyatt provided vocals to a recording of John Cage's 'The Wonderful Widow of Eighteen Springs', a piece based on a page of *Finnegans Wake*, and he has collaborated with the jazz composer Michael Mantler on settings of texts by Edward Gorey, Harold Pinter and Paul Auster.[28]

As can clearly be seen, Wyatt relates to a long, connective history of artists who have placed the sounds of sense and nonsense at the heart of their work.[29] This relationship only deepens the further one investigates Wyatt's discography. His contribution to Morgan Fisher's 1980 album *Miniatures*, for example, finds him sharing groove space with Bob Cobbing, Henri Chopin, Ivor Cutler and George Melly (the latter reciting the *Ursonate*). Fisher's project consists of '51 tiny masterpieces', each around a minute in length, edited into 'bands'. Wyatt provides a snippet of him singing the Frank Sinatra classic 'Strangers in the Night' which has been looped and repeated until it leads, like Brion Gysin's permutated poems or Steve Reich's tape experiments, to a breakdown in semantic sense. The resulting piece is titled 'rangers in the nightst' as a way of reflecting the reformulated phonemes, another signal of the difficulty of matching the written word against the sounded word.[30]

Wyatt's interest in the relationship between words, music and meaning can also be detected in his devotion to jazz. As a form of musicking, a way of processing musical language, jazz often places emphasis on the instrumentalization of the voice, most notable in the phenomenon of scat singing, but also present in the inflections and vocal experiments of most of the great jazz singers. Jazz acts as the constant in Wyatt's music, from his work with Soft Machine through collaborations with jazz musicians and the covering of jazz standards. His obsession with nonsensical singing and his love of what he calls 'a good tune' are both connected to this tradition. The nonsensical side is displayed in a collaboration with Gilad Atzmon on the latter's composition 'Re-arranging the 20th Century', where Wyatt provides a spoken contribution that fuses his typical whimsy with the tradition of jive language associated with jazz: 'In the beginning was the bird and the bird was bop. That's bebop, short for Beelzebop.'[31] The love of a good tune, meanwhile, is amply demonstrated on '... *for the ghosts within*', a collaboration between Wyatt, Atzmon and Ros Stephen, on which half the songs are jazz standards or pop songs indelibly associated with jazz artists, such as 'Laura', 'Lush Life', 'In a Sentimental Mood' and 'Round Midnight'. Wyatt has claimed that he enjoys singing songs in other languages because it allows him a certain freedom from the words, giving him the opportunity to focus on singing. On '... *for the ghosts within*', Wyatt escapes the prison house of language by opting to whistle 'Round Midnight' and hum 'In a Sentimental Mood'. In the filmed interview that accompanied the album, Wyatt explains that words are unnecessary additions to some of the great jazz tunes and that, as a singer, he sometimes feels he gets the short straw. The whistling may be the logical extension of the ways in which, throughout his career, he has explored the interaction of words, language, sound and sense by using deliberately absurdist techniques. But the voice-as-instrument is also a voice that delivers messages and asserts a shared humanity.

Googa Mooga

The voice, in its ability to act as instrument and carrier of verbal messages, offers scope for singers and songwriters to work with different layers of meaning when it comes to the use of words and word-like elements in songs. This can lead to the use of coded language as a mode of subversion but it can also allow for verbal and vocal pleasure and play, the chance to explore what Brandon LaBelle calls 'the choreographies of the mouth'.[32] Part of this pleasure can be found in the use of infantile language as a way of holding onto or returning to supposedly innocent states. In his study of the use of childlike language in pop songs, Nadav Appel argues that the use of silly words provides a way of emphasizing the communicative potential of songs:

It is not as if the songwriters could not think of 'real' words, words with a designated sense, and had to settle for something that sounds 'like a word', but vice versa. At the peak moment of these songs ... words with ordinary, conventional sense just cannot produce the right effect. They cannot 'speak for themselves', since they are chained to sense. Only through baby talk, the becoming-child of language or the becoming-child in language, is it possible to liberate the expressive material that some songs' zenith requires.[33]

For Appel, it is important to emphasize the play, pleasure and rightness of such nonsense words in pop rather than always recuperate them into narratives of rebellion or resistance. Musicians as varied as Larry Williams, Little Richard, Gene Vincent, the Crystals, the Beatles, the Spice Girls, Sigur Rós, Diamanda Galás, Björk and Lady Gaga provide examples of the 'becoming-child' of language and of the process of savouring words for their sonic potential.

To begin our survey of some of these uses of words and almost-words, let's consider how a simple blurring between these categories can occur merely from the pairing of certain words. The sound of words working together in rhythm, rhyme and harmony is crucial, as is the effect each word has on its other(s). As Susan Stewart writes,

When we hear rhyme shmyme, helter-skelter, fender bender, double trouble, mishmash, hoity-toity, flimflam, dingdong, or such ancient examples as hoi polloi and holy moly, we are in the realm of instant parody. The reason for that, it seems, is the universal principle that the closer rhymes appear as adjacent pairs, the stronger the sound play and lesser the stability of meaning in individual words. These mnemonics are literal models of equivocation; the second term modifies and weakens the force of the first as our attention is drawn to sound alone.[34]

Stewart is discussing poetic rhyme but it is striking how her list of examples sounds like a catalogue of pop song titles. 'Helter Skelter', of course, was a Beatles song and has been covered by many other artists. Little Richard's 'Tutti Frutti' would fit Stewart's list, as would many of the songs included on *Great Googa Mooga!*, a compilation released by Ace Records in 2003. Curators Herb Fenstein and Brian Nevill take their title from a song released by Tom & Jerrio in 1965; other tracks included on the CD include Larry Williams's 'Heeby Jeebies', the Penguins' 'Ookey Ook', Pretty Boy's 'Bip Bop Bip' and the Bobbettes' 'Um Bow Bow'.[35] As well as hearing the parody that Stewart highlights, repeated sounds provide a dynamism to song titles and lyrics; it's no coincidence that many novelty song titles refer to dances: the Vibrations' 'The Watusi'; the Coasters' 'Little Egypt (Ying-Yang)'; Huey 'Piano' Smith's 'Rockin' Pneumonia and the Boogie Woogie Flu'. Wilson Pickett's 1966 smash hit 'Land of 1000 Dances' consisted of a list of dances – the Pony, the Chicken, the Mashed Potato, the Alligator, the Watusi, the Twist, the Fly, the Jerk, the Tango, the Yo-Yo, the Sweet Pea, the Hand Jive, the Slop, the Bop, the Fish, and the Popeye – interrupted by the wordless refrain 'na-na-na-na-na na-na-na-na-na-na-na-na'. The focus on dance, along with the closely paired lyrics ('Got to know how to pony / Like Bony Maronie / Mashed potato / Do the alligator') highlight the dynamic vitality of nonsense for pop, as well as the magical, ritual use of nonsense for affective processes. Nonsensical outbursts such as Little Richard's 'Awopbopaloobop alopbamboom' (the opening and refrain of 'Tutti Frutti') are, as much as anything, a conjuring of the dance-primed body.[36]

Dancing has often featured in nonsense literature as a way of bringing together verbal and physical play. In Margaret Mahy's 'The Man from the Land of Fandango', dancing unites humans, birds and beasts as 'bears and bison join in / And baboons with bassoons make a musical sound'. The fandango can even raise the long-dead: 'the dinosaurs join the din / And they tingle and tongle and tangle / Till tomorrow turns into today'.[37] Just as there is freedom in the realms of nonsense and beyonsense, in the Futurists' *parole in libertà*, or in Julian Ríos's *liberature*, so too is freedom summoned by the exuberantly articulated nonsense syllables of dance songs: the freedom of uninhibited expression, of play, of cutting loose and indulging in the excitement of new experiences. The vitality and dynamism of nonsense-related words and sounds also cause other types of dancing, such as that of the vocal apparatus as speakers give themselves over to the pleasures and challenges of voicing silly sounds, or that of the dancing ear of the listener.

'Skid-Dat-De-Dat'

As Thomas Brothers makes clear in *Louis Armstrong: Master of Modernism*, Armstrong was by no means the first to perform scat singing on record; precursors include Gene Greene's 1911 and 1917 recordings of 'King of the Bungaloos', as well as various recordings by Ukulele Ike (Cliff Edwards) and Don Redman.[38] Even so, Armstrong's 1926 recording of 'Heebie Jeebies' would become a landmark example of scat, enhanced by the often-told story of Armstrong dropping his lyric sheet during the recording and deciding to extemporize so as not to waste the take. While this account emphasizes Armstrong's resourcefulness, it must be complemented with awareness that he and his fellow musicians had been exposed to scat techniques for some years, often as ways of approximating musical instruments. This is worth highlighting because it serves as a reminder of the many longstanding musical traditions where non-semantic vocables are used for solmization or to approximate musical instruments other than the voice; in addition to scat, examples include Celtic *puirt à beul*, Sami *joik*, Indian *bol* and Japanese *shoga*.[39] Each tradition has its own histories and William Bauer sketches a useful one for scat, taking in Leo Watson, Armstrong, Cab Calloway, Ella Fitzgerald, Slim Gaillard, Dizzy Gillespie, Kenny Hagood, Sarah Vaughan, Betty Carter, Al Jarreau and Bobby McFerrin. Crucial to Bauer's analysis of Armstrong and Carter in particular is the development of new vocabularies of scat, such that particular syllables can be associated with eras in the music's history.[40]

Scat is an evolving language and not an absolute musical system where particular syllables relate to fixed instruments, melodies, rhythms or styles. This fluidity maps onto the blurred relationship scat syllables have with words, evident in Armstrong's shift from song lyrics to nonsense syllables in 'Heebie Jeebies'. Other Armstrong tracks, such as 'Skid-Dat-De-Dat' and 'Hotter than That', are instrumentals with scatted interludes; because there are no verses or chorus there is less of a temptation to hear the vocables as moving towards or away from regular words than in 'Heebie Jeebies'.[41] However, the partial transcription of Armstrong's scat as the title for the first track offers an invitation to make words of the vocables; so too with attempts to transcribe scat solos, such as Mezz Mezzrow's for 'Heebie Jeebies' and Barry Kernfeld's for 'Hotter than That'. Introducing the latter, Kernfeld refers to 'the outpouring of an irresistibly joyful private language'.[42] Bauer, who offers his own transcriptions for 'Heebie Jeebies', 'Hotter than That' and Betty Carter's scat on 'Babe's Blues', makes a connection between Carter's scat syllables and the subject matter of the song: 'Jon Hendricks's witty lyrics to the song implicitly encourage listeners to be as hip as children – who, "unlike adults," take life's hardships in stride. Hendricks's text serves largely to set an ironic, detached tone consistent with the bop aesthetic. In some ways, the nonsense syllables of Carter's scat solo also suggest a cool version of baby talk'.[43]

Another area of jazz singing connected to nonsense is the vocalese of artists such as Eddie Jefferson, Jon Hendricks, King Pleasure and Annie Ross, all famous for setting new words to existing melodies of jazz instrumentals and instrumental solos. While many of their lyrics were semantically logical and often devoid of scat's nonsense syllables, the imitation of instruments led to melodic contours which were not always amenable to easy comprehension of lyrics. In the liner notes to an album shared by King Pleasure and Annie Ross, Ira Gitler notes the saxophone solo as a favourite sound to be imitated due to its role as 'the human voice of all instruments'. Gitler places Pleasure and Ross in a lineage that includes Armstrong's scat, Leo Watson's stream-of-consciousness singing, Slim Gaillard's 'inanities' and the vocal experiments of Dizzy Gillespie, Dave Lambert and Babs Gonzales.[44] Ira Steingrout tells a similar story with regard to Eddie Jefferson, while making a stronger claim for Jefferson as an originator. Steingrout also makes the important connection to other art worlds too when he writes 'what's most striking about Eddie's early creativity is his repeated statement that (like Dada, surrealism or bop itself) it was private and done basically for the kicks it gave him and his friends'.[45] As well as forging a relationship like those I am pursuing in this book (a relationship underlined by *Time*'s description of Lambert, Hendricks and Ross as 'the James Joyces of jive'), Steingrout's take on Jefferson resonates with notions of jazz as a coded language and with nonsense as a private or domestic language.[46] Jazz vocalese also had an influence on other areas of popular music, for example in Van Morrison's professed debt to King Pleasure and Joni Mitchell's cover version of Annie Ross's 'Twisted'.

Slim Gaillard's use of nonsense language is distinctive in comparison with his peers in that he would use his invented words during regular speech; he even had his own language, Vout-o-Reenee, for which he wrote a small dictionary. Vout and other bebop-flavoured terms would appear in his songs, including 'Vout Orenee' (1945), 'Poppity Pop' (1945), 'Cement Mixer' (1945) 'Opera in Vout' (1946), 'Arabian Boogie' (1947) and 'Soony-Roony' (1951). Gaillard was immortalized speaking Vout in Jack Kerouac's *On the Road*, and one of the episodes of a four-part film made about Gaillard in 1989 shows Van Morrison reading the extract from Kerouac's novel while Gaillard plays bongos. Another features a conversation between Gaillard and Dizzy Gillespie in which the two jazz veterans discuss the language of bebop and how nonsense syllables were used as communicative devices between musicians from different linguistic cultures. While the bebop terms that Gillespie uses translated mostly to instrumental tones and textures, Gaillard's Vout-O-Reenee matched nonsense syllables to English words, as becomes evident when he starts to read from his dictionary (mo-leev-ef = pencil, money seal = silver, moo-o-kee = cow, moo-row = roast beef). This and the shots of Gaillard with a cement mixer ensure that real-world referents are available throughout the four-hour film even as it's soundtracked with sounds of nonsense.[47]

'Hada-Looda-Turkey-Too'

Much of the research done around non-lexical vocals in music is concerned with transcription and pedagogy and makes the case for each system being sensical in its own context even as it is nonsensical to non-initiates. David Hughes uses the term 'acoustic-iconic mnemonic systems' to describe vocables used in a variety of global music cultures as 'this reflects the fact that certain phonetic features of the syllables – both vowels and consonants – are in an iconic relation to the musical sounds they represent; that is, they mimic or resemble them closely acoustically, as onomatopoeic words imitate sounds'.[48] Meanwhile, from the world of literary studies, Marnie Parsons provides an analysis of work by Louis Zukofsky that dwells on the relationship between musical and verbal coherence. Dealing as she is with a poet, her focus is on how the musicality of words adds extra meaning to their semantic content, becoming 'a movement of sounds in performance'. Non-semantic vocables in music offer the reverse process, whereby words primarily used for musical qualities might also work as carriers of proto-semantic content. Yet I might come to a conclusion similar to Parsons's when she notes that 'words don't *become* music, nor music words; the one doesn't cancel the other out. Rather the ear comes to negotiate a delicate balance between music and language.'[49] It is in this negotiation, this delicate balance, that one may wonder where sense-making is happening; non-lexical vocables may not become words, but they may provide enough in the way of phonemic, morphemic and semantemic elements for the mixing desk of the ear to produce an attempt at semantic meaning, an attempt that is crucially thwarted and therefore reaches the listener as a kind of nonsense.

A similar blurring can be detected in some types of yodelling. Timothy Wise has helpfully categorized yodels into a series of types, using the notion of the 'yodeleme' as a primary unit of meaning. First species yodelling is where only nonsense syllables pertain, with no attempt to form words. Second species, which Wise also refers to as 'word-breaking', occurs when one or more yodelemes are inserted into a word while it is being sung; Wise uses the example of Kenny Roberts's 'Broken Teenage Heart', where the word 'easy' is broken by a two yodelemes on the first syllable, which delay the resolution of the word.[50] As I understand Wise's typology, the distinction between first and second species yodels might be thought of as analogous to that between the scatted parts of a jazz song and those parts which employ regular singing of words with occasional vocal adornments; one presents a system with its own musicological rules, while the other stages a more obvious interruption into the sense-making processes of the voiced lyric. Often the lines blur. To take an example from my own listening history, at the end of Butch Hancock's 1978 recording of 'West Texas Waltz' there is a yodel of around fifteen seconds' duration. It is delivered in two parts, with the end of each string of nonsense syllables resolving with regular-sounding words; the second half runs something like 'ada-looda-lubba-gada-lay-eeee-ada-lay-ee-ada-lay-eeee-ada-looda-lidda-lev-a-level-and-a-lidda-hada-looda-turkey-too'.[51] The 'turkey' always stands out for me, both for the humour in hearing it and for the way in which Hancock wrenches extreme nonsense back to only partial nonsense, as if needing to finish the song with a regular English word or two. But it also serves as a reminder of the easy slippage between the non-lexical and the lexical.

If second species yodelling presents us with one form of word mutation, another can be found in the strange concoctions of Shirley Ellis. Ellis made a speciality of novelty songs that played on the kind of nonsense games favoured by children, such as 'The Clapping Song', 'The Nitty Gritty', 'The Name Game' and 'The Puzzle Song'. There was often a governing logic to the nonsense. In 'The Name Game', a complex set of rules are used to create rhyming words for any given name. Both the rules and the results are given within the song itself, making for a confusing but enjoyable sound text. The first letter of the name is replaced with B, F or M and prefixed with 'bo', 'fo' or 'mo' and the nonsense sounds 'na-na' and 'fee fi' are added. The song starts with the game being applied to Ellis's own first name: 'Bo-ber-ley bo-na-na fanna / Fo-fer-ley fee fi mo-mer-ley Shirley!' The result is rather like a verse from Edward Lear's nonsense alphabets. The use of this much-covered song in an episode of the television series *American Horror Show* offers an example of the proximity between nonsense and mental illness as asylum patients are seen singing and dancing along to a version sung by Sister Jude / Judy (Jessica Lange) following her return from electroshock treatment. Other Ellis song games include 'Ever See a Diver Kiss His Wife While the Bubbles Bounce About Above the Water', which found her playing with the words from the refrain by singing 'Did you ever-eever-eyever in your life-lee-low / See a diver-deever-devver kiss his wife-wee-woe'.[52]

'The Bomp in the Bomp Bomp Bomp'

Like scatting and vocalese, doo-wop offers an example of singers emulating instruments while also giving an insight into the relationship between semantic and non-semantic voicing. The genre developed in the period following the Second World War but flourished mostly in the 1950s and 1960s, peaking around 1960–1 before fading somewhat with the ascendancy of beat groups and new directions in soul music. Many of the notable 1960s soul artists began careers in gospel or doo-wop groups and the harmonies found in doo-wop songs can be found in numerous vocal groups of the

Motown era. Doo-wop can be connected to earlier, longstanding traditions such as gospel and barbershop groups, where voices pitched to different registers combine to form harmonically rich and thick textures. While doo-wop was the favoured style of groups (often teenagers) without access to musical instruments, doo-wop as a commercial genre often had instrumental accompaniment. Even then, voices predominated, with sung lines complemented by the kind of repeated refrains that would become a staple of back-up singers in multiple genres and, crucially, nonsense syllables such as 'do', 'da', 'did', 'sha', 'wah', 'dee', 'rama', 'shanga', 'lama', 'la', 'be', 'bop', 'ding', 'dong', 'dooby' and so on. Combinations of these sounds proliferated among groups such as the Dominoes, the Clovers, the Du Droppers, the Royals, the Penguins, the Diamonds, the Belmonts, the Fleetwoods, the Drifters, the Miracles and the Rivingtons.[53] Not surprisingly, elements from aesthetically and/or commercially successful songs were picked up and repurposed for new songs, both as a way of establishing an effective grammar of doo-wop and as a way of achieving fame and possible fortune. The famous bass riff introduction to the Marcels' hit version of 'Blue Moon', for example, was taken from the Collegians' 'Zoom Zoom Zoom', a single from 1958. For their follow-up 'Heartaches', the group employed a very similar string of nonsense syllables in a bass riff that had a comparable melodic contour. The seeming interchangeability of nonsense syllables in doo-wop led Bernard Gendron to use the genre as a case study for exploring – and ultimately refuting – the standardization thesis at the heart of Theodor Adorno's critique of popular music.[54]

We might see the reuse of nonsense strings in doo-wop and doo-wop-influenced music as a recognition of a shared grammar of sublime expressivity, a mildly subversive coded language, and an imitative process central to what Nadav Appel calls the 'becoming-child' of pop-rock singing. Lawrence Pitilli, who describes doo-wop nonsense syllables as 'logatomes' (after the units used by Ebbinghaus), sees them as aiding the coming-together of young people searching for their own language:

> the use of doo-wop logatomes were not carefully engineered efforts on the part of record producers or doo-wop-group lead singers to create a new sound in popular music. Rather they reflected the inherent attention-grabbing playfulness of language

and its accompanying sound production, particularly when musically embedded in a youth culture not atypically struggling to find its own voice (and one might argue its own words and sounds).[55]

The notion of having a language of one's own is important to many subcultures and the slang and codes of subcultural groups provide examples of the kind of nonsense that is only nonsensical to outsiders. At the same time, Pitilli's focus on play is important and resonates with Appel's arguments regarding childlike language as the playful 'zenith' of many popular songs. These zeniths provide the vitality of many songs, both in terms of giving singers and listeners memorable elements for participation and by providing lasting historical resonance and the conditions for recuperation.

Barry Mann's 1961 song 'Who Put the Bomp (in the Bomp, Bomp, Bomp)' might be thought of as a meta-doo-wop piece in that it looks reverentially and referentially back at the doo-wop era while also participating in its ongoing history. Working in collaboration with vocal group the Halos, Mann crafted a new doo-wop song by explicitly referencing past hits such as the Edsels' 'Rama Lama Ding Dong' (1958), the 'boogity boogity boogity boogity shoo' backing vocals of Chubby Checker's 'Pony Time' (1960) and the 'bomp ba bomp ba bomp' and 'dip da dip da dip' of the Marcels' 'Blue Moon' (1961). Historical resonance can be found in the song in part because it references hits of the past and in part because of the song's subsequent longevity through continued replay and cover versions. While the past that is referenced is a very recent one – 'Blue Moon' had only been released a matter of months before 'Who Put the Bomp' – it nevertheless provides a 'then' and 'now' for a lyric at once grateful and nostalgic: grateful because the singer is thanking the songwriter(s) who penned the hits 'that made my baby fall in love with me'; nostalgic because the song can also be heard as a paean from Mann the prolific songwriter to his admired predecessors and to an already passing golden era of doo-wop music.[56]

The move between semantic coherence and incoherence is key to the song. The question 'who put the "bomp" in the "bomp ba bomp ba bomp"?' makes sense on the semantic and syntactic as much as the phonic and musical levels. Similarly, use of the definite article singles out 'the bomp' and 'the ram' from what were otherwise nonsense noises ('bomp ba bomp ba bomp', 'rama lama ding dong'), making them seem more like real objects. At the same time, because of the proliferation of nonsense words and the fact that the non-nonsense words are single syllables, it is also easy to hear the words 'who' and 'put' as nonsense syllables, reducing the semantic logic again. There is no clear borderline between sense and nonsense here, but a dialectical play between them that also communicates strongly as a play of the lips and ears. This is further evident in a Spanish language version of the song released by Mexican rock 'n' roll imitators Los Teen Tops in 1961. Los Teen Tops' speciality was translated versions of American hits, such as 'El Rock De La Carcel' ('Jailhouse Rock'), 'Larguirucha Sally' ('Long Tall Sally'), 'Rey Criollo' ('King Creole') and 'Colina Azul' ('Blueberry Hill'). Often, as in their version of Little Richard's 'Tutti Frutti', the number of words to be translated was minimal due to the lack of English words in the original. Their version of Mann's song, 'Quien Puso El Bomp', likewise retains the original nonsense words and translates the standard English, with 'quien puso el' being placed in front of 'bomp ba bomp ba bomp', 'rama lama ding dong', and so on.

The many cover versions of 'Who Put the Bomp' have shown the persistent attraction for the song's nonsense, as it seems safe to assume that it is the doo-wop syllables of the chorus that have made the song memorable rather than the verses. This refusal to be fixed down can also be found in the song 'Surfin' Bird', released by the Trashmen in 1963. The song combined two earlier doo-wop songs by the Rivingtons, 'Papa-Oom-Mow-Mow' (1962) and 'The Bird's the Word' (1963). 'Papa-Oom-Mow-Mow' was built mainly on gibberish sounds, with the dominant bass riff of the title phrase complemented by a higher pitched 'papa papa oo-oo' and a staccato 'dit dit dit'. The verse played on this senselessness by referring to 'the funniest sound I ever heard / and I can't understand a single word', folding the novelty sounds into the narrative. 'The Bird's the Word' also alternated low and high register sounds, the repeated 'bird bird bird' bass riff set against falsetto screams and tweeting sounds, all at the service of promoting the titular dance. The Trashmen mashed the two songs together, simplifying them even further, so that the first minute of the song consists of variations on the line 'everybody's heard about the bird / bird bird bird b-b-bird's the word' 'don't you know about the bird?', followed by a brief meltdown/transition that provides the song with its title, and a further minute of 'papa oom mow mow' repeated over and over. The machine-gun delivery and repetition lend the recording a manic quality that marked the song as a proto-punk workout, something confirmed by the Ramones' subsequent cover version.[57]

As well as being covered by the Ramones and the Cramps, 'Surfin' Bird' has been used to soundtrack films and television programmes. A notable use of the song occurs in a 2008 episode of the animated show *Family Guy*. Main character Peter Griffin becomes the owner of a copy of the Trashmen's single after hearing it in a retro diner. He then proceeds to play and sing the song throughout the episode, to the annoyance of his family. One scene finds him in the kitchen with his son Stewie and dog Brian. Brian is reading a newspaper when Peter interrupts him:

> Peter: Brian, can I see that paper for a sec? [leafing through the paper] Huh, that's odd. I thought that would be big news.
> Brian: You thought what would be big news?
> Peter: There seems to be an absence of a certain ornithological piece, a headline regarding mass awareness of a certain avian variety.
> Brian: What are you talkin' about?
> Peter: Oh, have you not heard? It was my understanding that everyone had heard.
> Brian: 'Heard what?'

At this point, Peter launches into yet another rendition of 'Surfin' Bird', eventually collapsing in a fit on the kitchen floor. After a brief pause, during which Brian and Stewie express concern for his health, he jerks back to life and starts singing the 'papa oom mow mow' section. Here and in the rest of the episode – throughout which the Trashmen's song keeps recurring like the proverbial broken record – 'Surfin Bird' takes on the role of a viral life force, as if reversing its status as owned commodity by taking possession of its owner. In addition to placing this annoyingly catchy song into the minds of millions more people, the episode also illustrates the dialectic play of serious and silly by framing the illogical or irrational moments with the logical and rational. Here, nonsense is an irruption into the seemingly ordered world of normality.

A similar play of registers between the serious and the silly can be found in other framings of pop music with serious discourse. In a

1957 television broadcast, comedian Steve Allen mocked the lyrics of 'Be-Bop-a-Lula' by reciting them with as if they were Shakespearian verse, much to the amusement of his audience. In a 1969 episode of *Not Only ... But Also*, Dudley Moore was introduced as a 'coloured jazz singer' from America called Bo Dudley and was then asked by Peter Cook to translate the 'slang' of his song for an English audience. Both Cook and Bo/Moore speak in upper-class English accents, in deliberate contrast to Bo's American-inflected blues/soul growl when singing, and the humour relies on this play of registers as well as the ludicrous misinterpretation of the song lyrics. Decades later, in his programme 'The Joy of Gibberish', Stephen Fry provided a similar effect when, in his trademark posh voice, he mocked pop's nonsense language in a reference to 'the Eurovision Song Contest, with its vacuous pan-European boom-banga-langa-binga-babbly-babble-bop-a-lu-la'. In all these cases, it is the yoking together of mock seriousness, 'posh' accents and vernacular song lyrics that is designed to provoke humour.[58]

Yet, pop music has always been perfectly capable of mocking itself. In the melodramatic spoken section that appears partway through 'Who Put the Bomp', Barry Mann adopts an imploring tone to speak the words, 'Darling, bomp ba ba bomp, ba bomp ba bomp bomp, and rama langa ding dong forever'. In his 1988 song 'Tower of Song', Leonard Cohen mixes solemn and light-hearted observations, which are complemented by female backing singers chanting 'doo dum dum dum da doo dum dum'. In a 1993 interview, Cohen claimed that it was the addition of the nonsense syllables, created by his collaborator Jennifer Warnes, that 'nailed the song' and 'gave [it] the perspective of real humor'. In later concerts, Cohen would exaggerate the contrast between serious and silly by suggesting to his audience that he had uncovered 'the great mysteries' and 'penetrated to the very core of things', before revealing his discovery as 'da doo dum dum'.[59] This bringing forward of the backing vocals can also be found in Lou Reed's 'Walk on the Wild Side' where 'the coloured girls go doot di doot di doot doot di doot doot di doot ...'; such foregrounding alerts listeners to musical elements which more often go unremarked, as well as highlighting the gendered and racialized reasons why that might be so.[60] Backing vocals in pop songs are, of course, mostly meant to fade into the background (hence the name) and, like other non-lexical vocables mentioned in this chapter, are generally considered part of the musical texture provided by instrumental accompaniment to the leading voice. It is because of this instrumental role that the nonsense sounds (whether lexical or not) become more noticeable when they stop being sung and are foregrounded as spoken words or printed lyrics.

This prompts a few observations: that nonsense is less likely to go noticed when it is channelled into music; that what is nonsense in one mode is not in another, as musical sense-making takes over from semantic sense-making; and that, again, the nonsense moment can be thought of as that point where we are between these different sensical worlds. Whether in the exaggerated nonsense of the *Family Guy* episode and in the broadcasts of Allen, Cook, Moore and Fry, or in the humorous melodrama of Mann's and Cohen's songs, such explicit foregrounding highlights the nonsense moment as we are asked to code-switch between spoken verbal semantics and their musico-nonsensical counterparts. It is this bringing forth of the nonsense moment that justifies for me the connection between musical nonsense and the other nonsense worlds discussed in this book.

I am not alone in highlighting such connections. Speaking about his love of doo-wop bass voices, musician Ezra Furman says 'There's something almost – the nonsense of it – avant-garde in them, like Dadaism. Salvador Dali might have liked doowop a lot'.[61] This connection is pursued at greater length by the Canadian 'soundsinger' Paul Dutton, who created a performance piece and an essay both entitled 'Beyond Doo-Wop or How I Came to Realize that Hank Williams is Avant-Garde'. Dutton describes the performance as follows:

> A brief ad-libbed tribute to doo-wop bass singers forms the starting point for a free voice improvisation that follows its nose (sometimes literally) through a series of effects, including mouth percussion, vocalizing through lip-flutters, inhaled singing, closed-throat singing, an inversion of the two opening parts, and a few other devices, finishing with an ad-libbed diphonic mock country-and-western melody, the nasal resonance gradually removed, to let the purer tone prevail at the end.[62]

Dutton's piece does indeed traverse all these sonic, generic and physical territories and is a tour-de-force not only of what Dutton calls 'soundsinging' (a term he prefers to 'sound poetry'), but also of the tangled interconnections between vernacular and art practice, conjoining the bass riffs and logatomes of groups such as the Marcels and the high lonesome yodelemes of country singers to the vocal experiments of artists such as Hugo Ball, Kurt Schwitters, Bob Cobbing, Steve McCaffery and Jaap Blonk.[63] In his article of the same name, Dutton notes this conjuncture by describing his feelings at hearing 'art-music diva' Diamanda Galás performing Screamin' Jay Hawkins's classic 'I Put a Spell on You'. He refers to his longstanding fascination with doo-wop bass voices, 'the elastic-lipped, tongue-rattling sensuality of the sounds, my senses stirred by nonsense'. As with his performance of 'Beyond Doo-Wop', the article finds multiple connections across twentieth-century sonic arts that blur the boundaries between the avant-garde and vernacular, making the case for sonic nonsense as an arena where categorizations start to crumble. Dutton also recounts the development of his own work, going into technical detail about diphonic and multiphonic vocal styles and locating them in work by Peter Maxwell Davies, Little Richard, Clarence 'Frogman' Henry, Mongolian *hoomi* singing, and Hank Williams's 'Honky Tonkin'.[64]

Christian Bök similarly draws comparisons between avant-garde and pop artists while making a point that relates to John Giorno's observations about poets becoming rock musicians. Speaking in 2005, the example he uses is beatboxing:

> To me, the more virtuoso work is taking place among people who are doing musical mimicry, like the vocal percussionists. Rahzel or Dokaka are quite exceptional performers who make avant-garde practitioners look completely naive by comparison. It's amazing how such beat-boxers can upstage other performers in athleticism and complexity. They are truly incredible. That's why I feel obliged to learn that particular skill set: in order to expand my repertoire as a sound poet. I do it as a matter of course. I want to try to sustain this kind of practice; that's one of the fertile avenues of exploration. It seems to me that those kinds of people in pop music – people whom you might hear on Björk's most recent album *Medulla* – might be poets more so than musicians, although they're functioning in a totally different, artistic universe.[65]

Beatboxing, like scat, vocalese, doo-wop and backing vocals, is a technology of imitation, yet generally relies less on elements that might be heard as words or nonsense syllables due to its focus on much shorter sonic units (beats, scratches, bass notes, sampler sounds). However, some artists – including Bök's example, Rahzel – have perfected the art of beatboxing and rapping/singing simultaneously, meaning that sensible lyrics or lyrical fragments are mixed with instrumental imitation in a sonic palimpsest. Other examples can be found in the popular YouTube videos of Nicole Paris and Eklips, while musician and comedian Reggie Watts performs sets that mix surreal stand-up comedy, beatboxing and singing and that often involve significant elements of gibberish.[66]

Where beatboxing does bring in word fragments, it is often as a reminder of the importance of sampled and manipulated elements in the hip-hop sound mix. Rapping, meanwhile, connects to a lineage of black vernacular practices that have often embraced childlike and nonsensical elements. As with other musical styles discussed in this chapter, non-lexical elements often come to the fore when the musicality of speech is being highlighted. The 1979 track 'Rapper's Delight' inaugurated hip-hop's mainstream crossover success with the lines 'I said a hip hop the hippie the hippie to the hip hip hop and you don't stop / The rock it to the bang bang boogie say up jump the boogie to the rhythm of the boogie, the beat'. The title alerted listeners to the pleasure in wordplay and the song – especially in its fourteen-minute version – bore this out over multiple inventive rhymes. The rhythm of the rap is vital to the affect of the music, focused as it is on getting people to dance ('me, the groove, and my friends are gonna try to move your feet'). We find a similar process in another old-school classic, Busy Bee's 'Making Cash Money' (1982), which benefits additionally from a nonsense refrain that has a passing resemblance to the bass riff of The Marcels' 'Blue Moon'.[67]

The musicality of rhyming in old-school party hip-hop might make us wonder why sensible words – which form the main body of 'Rapper's Delight', interspersed with further non-lexical combinations – are even necessary. Commenting on originality and authenticity in the early days of hip-hop, MC Grandmaster Caz (Curtis Fisher, aka Casanova Fly) has pointed out that the lyrics for 'Rapper's Delight' rapped by Big Bank Hank (Henry Lee Jackson) were plagiarized from his (Caz's) notebooks and not even changed to reflect the rappers' different names, as can be heard when Jackson raps 'I'm the C-A-S-A, the N-O-V-A, And the rest is F-L-Y'. Semantic sense seems to be less important here than the flow of the sounds. Meanwhile, as Sujatha Fernandes notes, the swift global success of 'Rapper's Delight' was based more on phonological sense than semantics, with many non-English speakers confused by the lyrics. An early response song by the Venezuelan comedian Pedro 'Perucho' Conde, entitled 'La Catorra Criolla', positions the foreign track as parrot-like babble, while the bizarre 'Rapper's Deutsch' by G.L.S.-United (a group made up of German TV celebrities) recasts the song as a history of rock and pop acts (mostly British and American, with a sprinkling of German artists) 'rapped' in German but relying on English band names.

Turning the tables, it's worth also noting that rappers have responded to other musical genres in similar ways, such as when DMC (Darryl McDaniels), of pioneering group Run-DMC, describes the lyrics to 'Walk this Way', by 1970s rockers Aerosmith, as 'hillbilly gibberish'.[68] Despite such reservations, the two groups collaborated on a rock-rap version of the song that became a massive hit in 1986. The video that accompanied the single dramatized the supposed 'war' between rap and rock, portraying the two groups as noisy neighbours with distinct listening communities, ultimately united through the alliance of Run-DMC and Aerosmith. This and the musical mash-up of 'Walk this Way' suggested that musical languages developed in isolation from each other can merge in the musical palimpsest. But this isolation was never absolute; Aerosmith's music, like that of the Rolling Stones before them, was rooted in African American traditions, particularly the blues, while the hip-hop culture from which Run-DMC emerged was as reliant on rock music textures and aesthetics as it was on those of other musical genres.

From a sense-making perspective, the important aspect here is the ability of words and/as sounds to translate from one cultural space to another. Another example of this is the 1984 single 'Cockney Translation' by reggae toaster Smiley Culture, which offers equivalencies between Cockney slang and Jamaican patois. While the track makes conventional (semantic) sense and has a structuring logic that is easy to follow, it still presents itself as a coded sonic text, one which will not give up its meaning as easily as another in more 'standard' English, hence the need for translation between two specialist linguistic systems. A similar case can be found in 'Ebonics', a 1998 single by US rapper Big L, which translates African American vernacular language into then-mainstream American English, yet does so at such a lightning rate that it risks the danger of continued misunderstanding. In 'Slang Like This', released by True Tiger in 2011, British grime MC P Money repeats a string of slang terms ('bredrin cuz bredrin bradda bredrin safe bredrin'), many of which have come to the UK from the Caribbean. Far from being about exclusivity, P Money argues that slang is what brings different audiences together around his music and this sense of community is echoed in the song's video, in which a diverse range of people are seen mouthing the lyrics. A version of the song by north-east-based rapper Aems, entitled 'Geordie Slang Like This' attempts a similar strategy, with a video showing people from the Newcastle area mouthing the Geordie terms.[69]

Slang designates roots and routes as terminology migrates across time and space. Wayne Marshall provides a detailed example of this in his ongoing study of 'the zigzagging zunguzung meme'. Marshall traces the various usages of the nonsense phrase 'Zungguzungguguzungguzeng' and its accompanying melody since its appearance on a recording of the same name by reggae artist Yellowman in 1982. As Marshall shows, the continual re-emergence of the meme in reggae, hip-hop and reggaetón highlights the complex mutual influences between these musical cultures as well as the ways in which these musics offer self-reflection when artists historicize, theorize and pay tribute using musical fragments.[70] In terms of thinking about languages of the familiar and the unfamiliar, and of how we make sense of the world around us through language, a recent usage of the zunguzung meme by British grime MC Kano is illustrative; in his 2016 track 'New Banger', Kano includes the line 'Before I knew the whole alphabet / I knew Zungguzungguguzungguzeng'.[71]

A Tongue of One's Own

Slim Gaillard was not alone in his desire to create a new language in which to sing. Christian Vander of the French jazz-rock group Magma was another and he went even further than Gaillard, inventing a history of a people called Kobaïans, named for the planet they settled after fleeing earth. Magma's music presents the mythology of this new culture, with lyrics written in the Kobaïan language. Vander based the language on Slavonic and German sounds but generally speaks of it as something he understands musically. In a 2015 interview looking back at his long career, he said, 'People used to say grudgingly that they liked Magma, but because of the Kobaïan they couldn't understand the words. And I said I liked Coltrane and I couldn't understand the words either.'[72] Despite the jazz reference, Kobaïan is not generally scat-like but tends more towards chanting, giving it an air of solemnity. A similar solemnity, and even melancholy, can be detected in the Vonlenska language (translated as Hopelandic) created by Icelandic post-rock group Sigur Rós. In his theorization of Hopelandic, Ethan Hayden makes reference to Hugo Ball, Kurt Schwitters, Christian Morgenstern and William Burroughs, as well as scat, doo-wop and vocalese. While these connections are analogous to the ones I am attempting in this book, I am also struck in Hayden's dissection of Sigur Rós by the emphasis placed on the blurriness of the vocals on many Sigur Rós tracks, which make them difficult to make out regardless of the language in which they're being sung.[73]

Sigur Rós are hardly alone here, as murky, mushy mixes abound in popular music; Edward Lear's evocation of 'melodious and mucilaginous sounds echoing all over the waters' may be an apt description for a broad range of pop aesthetics. The Cocteau Twins, often invoked as exemplars of indecipherable pop vocals, are remembered fondly by fans who speak of the inability to make out what Liz Fraser was singing. Stereolab are another group often lauded for indecipherability; in a review of the group's 2001 album *Sound-Dust*, Ken Hollings wrote that Lætitia Sadier and Mary Hansen 'no longer appear to be singing in any discernible language known to humanity', while other reviews made reference to nonsense and gibberish, even though the lyrics were all in English or French.[74] In an overview of singer-songwriter Tim Buckley's work, Ian Penman focused on the journey Buckley took from clear enunciation to non-semantic language: 'Starting with *Happy/Sad* (1968), on through *Blue Afternoon* (1969) and *Lorca* (1970), he planed down [his earlier] wordiness, until on *Starsailor* (1970) he jettisoned words altogether, and sang in some other language, some other tongue, like a Sun Ra of singer-songwriters'. Penman compares Buckley's singing to the playing of Albert Ayler and Eric Dolphy rather than singer-songwriter contemporaries, noting that

Buckley himself wanted to sound like John Coltrane: 'He sings the body etheric, rather than any earthbound song of introspection and plaint. He "sings" like other people send rockets to the moon.' When the Cocteau Twins' Liz Fraser, recording with This Mortal Coil, covered Buckley's 'Song to the Siren', it was perhaps only appropriate that she should decorate it with what Penman calls 'gilded gibberish'.[75]

To hear a singer famous for indecipherability perform a song by a singer fond of sailing beyond the safe shores of language is to be attuned to a very particular kind of bewilderment, one that offers no option but to give oneself over to the music of the voice. But gilded gibberish and murky mixes have perhaps taken us too far from the main route this chapter has been travelling. For the most part, I have not been discussing the clarity of the singing voice, but rather the language with which that voice is engaging. Whether focused on songwriting that has been strongly influenced by modernist literary aesthetics or on words and proto-words used by pop singers, I have been listening for a kind of nonsense that is (at least to my ears) not so far from that explored throughout the book. Nonsense, as a subject that gets studied (that is to say, taken seriously), remains a contentious field of study, yet I hope there is space in the discussion for the role of popular music within that field. I think there are various reasons why there is still some discomfort about this, both among those who take nonsense seriously and those who take popular music seriously. Regarding the former, it's worth considering the idea of nonsense as a deliberate strategy undertaken by privileged groups. For example, is one of the reasons why nonsense literature has been given preferential (even reverential) treatment in academia that it was mainly produced by educated *litterateurs* who knew 'better'? Is one of the problems with pop culture still that it is produced and consumed by those who don't (but should) know better? Pop music scholars, critics and fans know this not to be the case, yet we often perpetuate a different problem by letting our wish to take the music seriously manifest in a focus only on the serious. This can lead us to distrust play and pleasure and to forget the vital roles these have in what makes us love the music we love in the first place. In saying that I am absolutely not dismissing the important work done on showing how popular culture creates meaning, models community, amplifies resistance and sounds the specifics and the generalities of our society. On the contrary, having tried to do precisely that kind of work previously (and with plans to do more), I have occasionally felt conflict about devoting so much time to pop's play. But I believe that pop, like other art forms, responds to all of life's phenomena and does its work in many registers.

Conclusion: And the moral of *that* is…

Alice is told by the Duchess that if she watches the sense the sounds will take care of themselves. Others have suggested that, in fact, the Duchess's utterances make more sound than sense. But sounds make a sense of their own, especially sounds that are being 'watched'; a sonic narrative ensures that they are taken care of. Sounds do make sense but sound in this sense might better be thought of as another kind of sense. And if that sounds like the kind of nonsense utterance we might expect from the Duchess, then so be it. Sounds make sense and nonsense. By way of starting to reach a conclusion, then, let's think of nonsense as an interruption or irruption into a narrative mode. In Lewis Carroll's case, there is a narrative of the novel, or story, and then the nonsense disrupts the logical expectations of that mode, even as it contributes to the making of a new mode (nonsense literature), and what we come to value in nonsense literature is this moving between modes. So too in song, except that we have perhaps become more immune to the use of nonsense in music, where semantics often seem to be secondary anyway. Because there is a whole vocabulary of nonsensical – that is to say, non-semantic – sounds in song (hums, scats, broken, stretched, stressed and mutated syllables, stuttered consonants, open extended vowels, vocalese and so on), we notice this less than when weird words are written on the page. Far from impeding sense, these sounds constitute part (sometimes even all) of the narrative sense of the song. But does this mean that the song cannot be impeded by nonsense? Just as Carroll's nonsense disrupts the 'easy' flow of the fairy tale narrative while also being a vital part of that flow, so the constituent parts of voice-based music play multiple roles. Units that form the building blocks of communication – phonemes, morphemes, semantemes, memes, yodelemes, logatomes – combine with each other to build sense as well as interrupt it.

As to how nonsense sounds, there is no definitive answer, but I am drawn to requote Stephen Fry's description of Vivian Stanshall's voice as a way of thinking about and beyond the sound of nonsense. Stanshall's was a voice that 'reeks of Mullard valves covered in dust from old wireless sets and a sort of South Coast, vaguely colonial sense to it'. While attending to sound, there's also a wonderful synesthetic quality to Fry's description, evoking sight, smell, touch and the way that history feels. Is it worth thinking of nonsense, too, as an affront to all the senses and not just common sense (whatever that is)? I see no reason why not, especially if there can be nonsense botany (Lear's 'Bottlephorkia Spoonifolia'), cookery ('amblongus pie' – Lear again) and perfumery (Stanshall's 'sweet essence of giraffe'). In this book I have mostly stuck to what can be heard (in recited poetry of various sorts, and in music – mostly voice-based) and what can be heard in what is seen (the resonance of the page). But I have also alluded, in a way, to what can be tasted; on more than one occasion, I have highlighted the joy of having nonsense in the mouth. But what does nonsense taste like?

Nonsense is what's on the B-side of the platter, the sound of rainwater tinkling through the pink half of the drainpipe, the silly voice, the remix, the mash-up and the meme. It's the sound of falling down the rabbit-hole or passing through the looking-glass (Randy Greif has given us a good sense of what this sounds like, as have other musicians and sound designers). If it's not being fustian, it might be bluff and stiff-upper-lip and no-nonsense, but it's also common and coded and slangy. It's a play between registers, 'babellicose baabling', 'alphybettyformed verbage' that attempts to register 'the barking of Currs, bawling of Mastiffs, bleating of Sheep, prating of Parrets, tatling of Jackdaws, grunting of Swine, girning of Boars, yelping of Foxes'.[1] It's lists that flirt with the absurd, lists that flow, lists that list, flows that list (listen to Jesse Dangerously's 'Tom Lehrer's The Elements'[2]), listeners that flower and flowers that listen (nonsense botany again).

As Noel Malcolm discovered with nonsense literature, my sonic examples could be taken much further back in time. It may be useful to bear in mind some words from a talk given by Stanley Unwin on music, titled 'The Populode of the Musicolly':

> Please don't confuse or stretch the pigeonholes of your mind to encompass what these sounds really are. They do in fact go back

to Ethelrebbers Unready, King Albert's burnt capers where, you know, the toast fell in and the dear lady did get a very cross knit and smote him across the eardrome excallybold. The great sword which riseyhuff and Merlin forevermore was the beginning of the Great Constitution of the English-speaking peeploders of these islone, oh yes.[3]

The story of the sound(s) of nonsense can be taken as far back and as far abroad as one wishes, and is able, to go. There are places I haven't gone in this book, whether for lack of space, lack of adequate knowledge or oversight. Some of the sites I've tagged for future visits include comedy (only briefly covered here), opera, folk song, children's songs (Disney songs provide a tempting start: 'Bibbidi-Bobbidi-Boo', 'Supercalifragilisticexpialidocious', 'I Wanna Be Like You', 'Chim Chim Cher-ee') and the worldwide wonders of international gibberish. The latter invites the possibility of engaging in a kind of global *zaum*, of going 'beyonsense' beyond borders. In addition to locally and regionally understood nonsense cultures, there are also the routes taken when nonsense travels from one linguistic culture to another: the transnational transrational.[4]

Nonsense is a trail of temptations. Although I have only joined some of the audio dots and collected and connected just a sample of the sonic breadcrumbs, I have felt reassured in the alliances I have created by the knowledge that there is a wide community of watchers, listeners and browsers out there who keep alive the social life of nonsense. These are the people who, having stumbled for whatever reason on a YouTube video of Jaap Blonk performing Kurt Schwitters's *Ursonate*, make the mental leap to something they know better and post a link to John Larkin's 'Scatman (Ski Ba Bop Ba Dop Bop)'. New links are created by histories, likes, algorithms and yet more commenters, until you find yourself falling through the rabbit-hole into the Webland of 'Crazy Frog', 'The Gummy Bear Song', 'The Ketchup Song', 'Mr. Trololo', 'Rainbow Trololol', 'You're an Egghead', 'Octagon vs. Masked Hexagon' and 'Gangnam Bibi Hendl Style (Oppan Yodel Style Mashup)'.

Nonsense offers freedom not only from sense but from topic; it's often about deviation, about following a journey that twists and turns. This journey can also be thought of as a journey into sound, just like that promised by Coldcut on their 1987 remix of Eric B & Rakim's 'Paid in Full'; indeed, the journey into sound that is the remix is simultaneously a journey into nonsense, which itself, in its sonic unfolding, ushers in a new type of sense, one necessarily other than that of the original mix, possessed of its own internal logic. This book has modelled a tendency to deviation: a chapter ostensibly on written texts starts listening to films, audio recordings and musical responses; another on performed sound dwells on problems of transcription; a third on pop music looks for consonance in literature and experimental sound poetry. This is all part of the nonsense trail.

One possible outcome is that sound and nonsense rely on each other but in paradoxical ways. Sound is vital to the workings of nonsense even if the latter is encountered on the page, as we see in the importance given to phonics in Carroll and Lear. Yet when nonsense is sounded, it may escape the nonsensical by moving closer to a form recognized as music. Or rather, when nonsense is used as part of musical communication, the nonsensical may become less audible than it would in spoken communication. Or rather again, sonic nonsense becomes folded into musical communication so that it is hidden in ways it could not be in non-musical communication. Often we don't hear it, but when we listen for it we find it everywhere. As Laurence Sterne's Tristram Shandy might have it, 'It is the nature of an hypothesis, when once a man has conceived it, that it assimilates every thing to itself, as proper nourishment; and, from the first moment of your begetting it, it generally grows stronger by every thing you see, hear, read, or understand. This is of great use.'[5] I found this to be true while writing this book, though I tried not to be swayed by everything nonsensical I saw, heard, read or understood. There are many nonsense moments that I have tried to uncover here and I know they will not be recognizably nonsensical to all. I offer them anyway as sounds that I heard on the other side of sense.

Jean-Jacques Lecercle closes his *Philosophy through the Looking-Glass* with a self-reflexive concern about whether what he has written will itself be considered nonsense. He is thinking of that technical, critical use of the word 'nonsense' that is wielded, often by over-confident proclaimers of a particularly situated and disciplined line of reasoning, to blast those whose work and opinions they don't value. I am also interested in this slippage between nonsense literature and the way 'nonsense' is wielded as a weapon. Although I have not explored that relationship in depth here, it lurks not far beneath the surface of much of what I have been saying. *Philosophy through the Looking-Glass* itself is a model of clarity compared to some texts dealing with similar material. In reflecting on his methods and style, Lecercle discusses lucidity, contrasting the need for clear accounts with the various uses and abuses of *délire*. He speaks of the logophiles for whom linguistic play is part and parcel of their method (Saussure, Lacan and Deleuze are among those he lists; we might add Derrida). In praising rather than condemning such *déliristes*, Lecercle provides a powerful counterargument to 'no nonsense' naysayer critics.[6] Yes, *délire* can produce partial nonsense, a very valuable kind of nonsense that helps us think. Thought of this way, nonsense becomes a crucible in which new insight can be forged, a place of productive mutation and experimentation. I think of this as the vitality of nonsense, a vitality that enlivens pop culture as much as it does philosophy. Lecercle suggests that Deleuze, in his *Logic of Sense*, used writers such as Carroll not as examples but as philosophers, with literary texts provoking philosophical questions. While I have mostly designated my examples as examples in this book, I have also thought of the artists in question as theorists posing compelling questions (and sometimes providing answers) about sound, sense and meaning. Whether modernist, experimental, populist or a combination of all these elements, these artists all meet in the intersection of the nonsense moment.

In a later work, Lecercle discusses nonsense as a constant (back) ground from which sense is brought forward or out of. We might consider as analogous the relationship between noise, voice and speech, where noise is considered the ground of voice and speech. Because English (the language of the writers Lecercle is analysing) doesn't use all the 'licit' combinations of phonemes, nonsense takes up the slack. About Antonin Artaud, Lecercle writes, 'The object of nonsense is not the dissolution of all phonetic or phonological rules, but rather the mapping of them. Nonsense seeks to find out exactly what can be said, given the fact that not everything is actually said.' This stops Artaud (and presumably the Dadaists and many sound poets) being nonsense writers. Screams and related noises are absent from nonsense because 'nonsense texts explore articulate language' and deal with 'not merely word creation, but *regular* word formation'.[7] This seems a fair delimitation of nonsense *literature*, but we have moved beyond nonsense literature in this book. If I have persisted in making connections between nonsense writers, sound poets, musicians and other linguistic inventors, it is because I believe that a focus on the sonic requires it. The roping-off of nonsense into categories hides important connections, many of which are realized through sound, and it is these connections and those realizations that I have tried to reveal and record.

NOTES

Introduction

1 Lewis Carroll, *The Annotated Alice: Alice's Adventures in Wonderland & Through the Looking-Glass*, Definitive Edition, illus. John Tenniel, ed. Martin Gardner (New York: W. W. Norton, 2000), 92. Subsequent references to this work will be given in parentheses in the text as *AA*.

2 Mladen Dolar notes that the Duchess's words seem to be inverted, for her pronouncements, like many proverbs, 'make more sound than sense'; Mladen Dolar, *A Voice and Nothing More* (Cambridge, MA: The MIT Press, 2006), 147. Marnie Parsons begins her exploration of 'nonsense and sound' by quoting the Duchess and suggesting she 'was wrong, or partly wrong'; Marnie Parsons, *Touch Monkeys: Nonsense Strategies for Reading Twentieth-Century Poetry* (Toronto: University of Toronto Press, 1994), 120.

3 Parsons, *Touch Monkeys*.

4 Don Ihde, *Listening and Voice: Phenomenologies of Sound*, second edn (Albany: State University of New York Press, 2007), 4.

5 Christian Marclay, 'Music I've Seen: In Conversation with Frances Richard', in *On & By Christian Marclay*, ed. Jean-Pierre Criqui (London: Whitechapel Gallery, 2014), 85.

Chapter 1

1 Wim Tigges, *An Anatomy of Literary Nonsense* (Amsterdam: Rodopi, 1988).

2 I provide a partial but representative selection of the literature on nonsense in this chapter; for more detailed overviews of the critical commentary, readers are directed to the following as starting points: *Explorations in the Field of Nonsense*, ed. Wim Tigges (Amsterdam: Rodopi, 1987), in addition to the sources cited by

the various contributors, has an annotated bibliography by Tigges; Tigges's already cited *Anatomy of Literary Nonsense* expands on this considerably; Marnie Parsons's *Touch Monkeys: Nonsense Strategies for Reading Twentieth-Century Poetry* (Toronto: University of Toronto Press, 1994) allows for a broader nonsense remit than Tigges's works; *Nonsense and Other Senses: Regulated Absurdity in Literature*, ed. Elisabetta Tarantino and Carlo Caruso (Newcastle upon Tyne: Cambridge Scholars, 2009) expands the nonsense palette to include more international figures.

3 Elizabeth Sewell, *The Field of Nonsense* (London: Chatto and Windus, 1952), 1.

4 Jean-Jacques Lecercle, *Philosophy of Nonsense: The Intuitions of Victorian Nonsense Literature* (London: Routledge, 1994), 2.

5 Quoted in Robert Maslen, 'Introduction', in Mervyn Peake, *Complete Nonsense*, ed. Robert W. Maslen and G. Peter Winnington (Manchester: Carcanet, 2011), 4.

6 Ibid.

7 Michael Heyman, 'Introduction', in *The Tenth Rasa: An Anthology of Indian Nonsense*, ed. Michael Heyman, Sumanyu Satpathy and Anushka Ravishankar (New Delhi: Penguin, 2007), xx–xxi.

8 Noel Malcolm, *The Origins of English Nonsense* (London: Fontana, 1998), xvii–xviii.

9 Malcolm, *Origins*, 14–15.

10 Jacqueline Flescher, 'The Language of Nonsense in Alice', *Yale French Studies*, no. 43, The Child's Part (1969): 128.

11 Max Eastman quoted in Juliana Spahr's 'Afterword' to Gertrude Stein, *Tender Buttons*, Corrected Centennial Edition, ed. Seth Perlow (San Francisco: City Lights, 2014), 114. Adam Piette, *Remembering and the Sound of Words: Mallarmé, Proust, Joyce, Beckett* (Oxford: Clarendon Press, 1996), 11.

12 Lewis Carroll, *The Annotated Alice: Alice's Adventures in Wonderland & Through the Looking-Glass*, Definitive Edition, illus. John Tenniel, ed. Martin Gardner (New York: W. W. Norton, 2000), 124. Subsequent references to this work will be given in parentheses in the text as *AA*.

13 Stephen Fry, 'The Joy of Gibberish', *Fry's English Delight*, Season 2, ep. 4 (Audible download, 2010).

14 Jean-Jacques Lecercle, *Philosophy through the Looking-Glass: Language, Nonsense, Desire* (London: Hutchinson, 1985), 107.

15 Lecercle, *Looking-Glass*, 55.

16 Ibid., 77.
17 I'm thinking particularly of Ethan Hayden's book on Sigur Rós's
() (New York: Bloomsbury Academic, 2014), Stephen Fry's radio
programme on gibberish (cited above), the BBC documentary *Gaga
for Dada: The Original Art Rebels* (broadcast 21 September 2016),
presented by Jim Moir (aka Vic Reeves), and the BBC Radio 4
broadcast *Radio Dada* (1 October 2016), presented by Alexei Sayle;
each makes connections between different cultural practices, albeit
in different combinations: 'classic' nonsense literature, folk songs,
children's chants, jazz and popular music, Dada and sound poetry,
comedy. Marnie Parsons's already cited *Touch Monkeys* is one of the
most sustained scholarly accounts of sound and nonsense and makes
a broad range of connections between different art worlds. Prior to all
these examples, Susan Stewart's *Nonsense: Aspects of Intertextuality
in Folklore and Literature* (Baltimore: The Johns Hopkins University
Press, 1989) made a strong case for making connections across a
broad range of cultural practices and eras. Stewart's interest in the
intertextuality of nonsense is at times critiqued and at times ignored
in Wim Tigges's already cited works, which are sometimes careful to
remember their explicit focus on nonsense literature, and sometimes
not. In my broad approach to nonsense, I am closer to Stewart than
to Tigges.
18 Michael Heyman, *Isles of Boshen: Edward Lear's Literary
Nonsense in Context* (PhD Dissertation, University of Glasgow,
1999), 193.
19 Stewart, *Nonsense*, 3.
20 David Schwarz, *Listening Subjects: Music, Psychoanalysis, Culture*
(Durham: Duke University Press, 1997), 7–22.
21 James Rother, 'Modernism and the Nonsense Style', *Contemporary
Literature* 15, no. 2 (Spring 1974): 189. For Eliot's comparison of
music and poetry, see his *On Poetry and Poets* (London: Faber and
Faber, 1957), 26–38.
22 Heyman, *Isles of Boshen*, 221.
23 Douglas Kahn, *Noise, Water, Meat: A History of Sound in the Arts*
(Cambridge, MA: MIT Press, 1999), 40.
24 Ibid.
25 Jean-Luc Nancy, *Listening*, trans. Charlotte Mandell (New York: Fordham University Press, 2007), 6–7.
26 Parsons, *Touch Monkeys*, 22.
27 Heyman, 'Introduction', xxvii.

28 Velimir Khlebnikov, *Collected Works Volume I: Letters and Theoretical Writings*, trans. Paul Schmidt, ed. Charlotte Douglas (Cambridge, MA: Harvard University Press, 1987), 373.

29 Paul Schmidt, 'Translator's Preface', Velimir Khlebnikov, *Collected Works Volume III: Selected Poems*, trans. Paul Schmidt, ed. Ronald Vroon (Cambridge, MA: Harvard University Press, 1997), vii.

30 J.P. Das, 'Vain Cock', in Heyman, *The Tenth Rasa*, 96. Many texts in this collection mention the cawing of crows and ravens.

31 The Ivor Cutler Trio, 'Cockadoodledon't', *Ludo* (CD: Rev-Ola CRREV3, 2002).

32 Mikhail Bakhtin, *Rabelais and His World*, trans. Hélène Iswolsky (Bloomington: Indiana University Press: 1984), 317.

33 Don Ihde, *Listening and Voice: Phenomenologies of Sound*, second edition (Albany: State University of New York Press, 2007), 157; Sewell, *Field of Nonsense*, 2–3; Parsons, *Touch Monkeys*, 133–4.

34 Adriano Celentano, 'Prisencolinensinainciusol', *Nostalrock* (LP: Clan Celentano CLN 65764, 1973).

35 David Bellos, *Is That a Fish in Your Ear?: Translation and the Meaning of Everything* (London: Penguin, 2011), 43.

36 Bellos, *Is That a Fish*, 32.

37 See Umberto Eco, *Mouse or Rat?: Translation as Negotiation* (London: Weidenfeld & Nicolson, 2003).

38 Heyman, *Tenth Rasa*, xviii.

39 François Rabelais, *Gargantua*, trans. Andrew Brown (London: 100 Pages, 2003), 47–8. In his explanatory footnotes, Brown provides a more common English version: 'My argument is as follows: every bell that can be belled, belling in the belfry where belling takes place, in the bellative case makes bellable bells bell. Paris has bells. QED!' (146, n.85).

40 Stephen Rudy, 'Introduction' to Roman Jakobson, *My Futurist Years*, comp. and ed. Bengt Jangfeldt and Stephen Rudy (New York: Marsilio, 1997), xv.

41 'Blonk performs Ursonate with real-time typography', YouTube video uploaded 31 August 2008 by Golan Levin, https://www.youtube.com/watch?v=rs0yapSIRmM (last accessed 3 March 2017). Scatman John's 'Scatman (Ski-Ba-Bop-Ba-Dop-Bop)' can be found on his *Scatman's World* (CD: RCA 74321289942, 1995).

42 Watchmojo.com, '10 most hated songs', uploaded to YouTube 7 June 2014, https://www.youtube.com/watch?v=smTm7ESzc4k. Sample

quote: 'We know it's nonsense, we know it's garbage, but try going the rest of the day without humming it'. A sequel by the same team featured Black Eyed Peas 'Boom Boom Pow', Baha Boys' 'Who Let the Dogs Out' (animal noises), Ylvis's 'What Does the Fox Say?' (more animal noises) and 'I'm a Gummy Bear' ('helium'/machine voices, with versions in twenty languages apparently) and Psy's 'Gangnam Style'. The lists didn't contain 'Scatman', even though the first one was a suggested video after Larkin's.

43 Jaap Blonk, 'Some words to Kurt Schwitters' URSONATE', Jaap Blonk's Web Pages, http://www.jaapblonk.com/Texts/ursonatewords.html (last accessed 3 March 2017).

Chapter 2

1 Marnie Parsons, *Touch Monkeys: Nonsense Strategies for Reading Twentieth-Century Poetry* (Toronto: University of Toronto Press, 1994), 128.

2 Jean-Jacques Lecercle, *Philosophy of Nonsense: The Intuitions of Victorian Nonsense Literature* (London: Routledge, 1994), 24 (my emphasis).

3 Robert Maslen, 'Introduction', in Mervyn Peake, *Complete Nonsense*, ed. Robert W. Maslen and G. Peter Winnington (Manchester: Carcanet, 2011), 4–5.

4 Lecercle, *Philosophy of Nonsense*, 2.

5 Edward Lear, 'The Scroobious Pip', in *The Complete Nonsense and Other Verse*, ed. Vivien Noakes (London: Penguin, 2006), 387–90. Further references to this work will be given in parentheses in the text as *CN*.

6 Lecercle, *Philosophy of Nonsense*, 21.

7 Lewis Carroll, *The Annotated Alice: Alice's Adventures in Wonderland & Through the Looking-Glass*, Definitive Edition, illus. John Tenniel, ed. Martin Gardner (New York: W. W. Norton, 2000), 150. Subsequent references to this work will be given in parentheses in the text as *AA*.

8 Lecercle, *Philosophy of Nonsense*, 22.

9 T.S. Eliot, 'The Music of Poetry', in *On Poetry and Poets* (London: Faber and Faber, 1957), 29.

10 Lecercle, *Philosophy of Nonsense*, 68; Elizabeth Sewell, *The Field of Nonsense* (London: Chatto and Windus, 1952), 17.

11 Sewell, *Field of Nonsense*, 18.
12 Vivien Noakes, Introduction to Lear, *Complete Nonsense*, xxv, xxiii–xxiv.
13 Jacqueline Flescher, 'The Language of Nonsense in *Alice*', *Yale French Studies*, no. 43, The Child's Part (1969): 129.
14 Flescher, 'Language of Nonsense', 130.
15 Francis Spufford, 'Introduction', in *The Chatto Book of Cabbages and Kings: Lists in Literature*, ed. Francis Spufford (London: Chatto & Windus, 1989), 5.
16 Ann Colley, 'Edward Lear's Limericks and the Reversals of Nonsense', *Victorian Poetry* 26, no. 3, Comic Verse (Autumn 1988): 295.
17 James Joyce, *Ulysses: The 1922 Text*, ed. Jeri Johnson (Oxford: Oxford University Press, 1998), 56. Further references to this work will be given in parentheses in the text as *U*.
18 Alan Shockley provides a useful overview of this literature as well as his own analysis of the music of *Ulysses* and *Finnegans Wake* in *Music in the Words: Musical Form and Counterpoint in the Twentieth-Century Novel* (Farnham: Ashgate, 2009).
19 Shockley, *Music in the Words*, 68.
20 Jeri Johnson, notes to Joyce, *Ulysses*, 875–6.
21 Eliot, 'Music of Poetry', 29.
22 Lecercle, *Philosophy of Nonsense*, 115; Johnson, notes to *Ulysses*, 876.
23 Hugh Kenner, *Joyce's Voices* (Berkeley: University of California Press, 1978), 18.
24 Julián Ríos, *Larva: Midsummer Night's Babel*, trans. Richard Alan Francis, Suzanne Jill Levine and Julián Ríos (London: Dalkey Archive, 2004), 12.
25 Whether unavoidable or manufactured, such techniques evoke haunting (and some would say hauntological) features as they lure listeners away from everyday speech and song. Philip Jeck's work is interesting here; hear, for example, *An Ark for the Listener* (CD: Touch, 2010) and see my review at *Tiny Mix Tapes* (6 October 2010), http://www.tinymixtapes.com/music-review/philip-jeck-ark-listener. On glitch, see Caleb Kelly, *Cracked Media: The Sound of Malfunction* (Cambridge, MA: MIT Press, 2009). On Joyce and radio, see James A. Connor, 'Radio Free Joyce: "Wake" Language and the Experience of Radio', *James Joyce Quarterly* 30, no. 4 / 31, no. 1 (1993): 825–43.
26 Steven Connor, *James Joyce* (Plymouth: Northcote House, 1996), 72.

27 See R. Brandon Kershner, *Joyce, Bakhtin, and Popular Literature: Chronicles of Disorder* (Chapel Hill: The University of North Carolina Press, 1989).
28 James Joyce, *Finnegans Wake* (London: Penguin, 2000), 3. Subsequent references to this work will be given in parentheses in the text as *FW*. On 'the linguistics of *délire*', see Jean-Jacques Lecercle, *Philosophy through the Looking-Glass: Language, Nonsense, Desire* (London: Hutchinson, 1985), 47–85.
29 Lecercle, *Looking-Glass*, 65.
30 Joseph Campbell and Henry Morton Robinson, *A Skeleton Key to Finnegans Wake: Unlocking James Joyce's Masterwork*, ed. Edmund L. Epstein (Novato: New World Library, 2013), 4. The section from which this quotation is drawn, 'Introduction to a Strange Subject', is reprinted in the liner notes to Patrick Ball, *Finnegans Wake* (CD, Celestial Harmonies 13113-2/13114-2, 1997).
31 Connor, *James Joyce*, 90, 95.
32 Ibid., 80.
33 Riós's novel *Casa Ulises* offers the most obvious example of this debt, structured as it is around Joyce's novel; see Julián Ríos, *The House of Ulysses*, trans. Nick Caistor (Champaign: Dalkey Archive, 2010). In an interview, Ríos cites Rabelais, Cervantes and Sterne as prime influences, with Joyce and O'Brien following closely behind. See Mark Thwaite, 'Interview with Julián Ríos', *Context*, no. 17 (n.d.), Dalkey Archive Press website, http://www.dalkeyarchive.com/interview-with-julian-rios (last accessed 3 March 2017).
34 Thwaite, 'Interview with Julián Ríos'.
35 Ríos, *Larva*, 51.
36 Thwaite, 'Interview with Julián Ríos'.
37 See the essays collected in *Audiobooks, Literature, and Sound Studies*, ed. Matthew Rubery (New York: Routledge, 2011).
38 Uncredited liner notes to *Alice in Wonderland*, ad. and prod. Douglas Cleverdon (LP, Argo. ZTA 501-2, 1958).
39 In recent years, a similar technique has been programmed into Siri, the voice recognition programme used in Apple smartphones; ask Siri to beatbox and he/she will start to repeat 'Boots and cats and boots and cats and boots and cats and boots and cats and boots'. These words are often used as ways to learn beatboxing. For an example, see the video 'Boots and Cats' uploaded to YouTube by Henry Edmonds on 23 January 2012, https://www.youtube.com/watch?v=Nni0rTLg5B8. The audio mix is by Robert Clouth.

40 Stow and Hepworth's film was silent of course, and musical accompanists, composers and sound designers have been providing soundtracks for it ever since.
41 Paul Mavis, review of *Alice in Wonderland* (dir. Jonathan Miller, BBC, 1966), DVD Talk (2 March 2010, http://www.dvdtalk.com/reviews/40635/alice-in-wonderland/ (accessed 30 March 2017).
42 Clare Kitson, DVD liner notes to *Alice*, dir. Jan Švankmajer, 1988 (DVD: BFI BFIB1095, 2011).
43 Randy Greif, quoted in Richard di Santo, 'Randy Greif: Through the Looking Glass', Incursion.org (10 August 2000), http://www.incursion.org/features/greif.html (accessed 3 March 2017).
44 Randy Greif, *Alice in Wonderland* (CD: Soleilmoon SOL 55, 2010).
45 Ogden's recording was made available by the Orthological Institute in association with the Gramophone Co. on a 78-rpm shellac disc (Cc 17594). It was also included on an album released by Folkways, *Meeting of James Joyce Society on October 23, 1951 Finnegan's Wake* (LP: Folkways FL 9594, 1960). It is widely available online. Ogden was the inventor of Basic English, a simplified form of the language used for instruction. Ogden and Joyce collaborated on a Basic English version of 'Anna Livia Plurabelle'. See Susan Shaw Sailer, 'Universalizing Languages: *Finnegans Wake* Meets Basic English', *James Joyce Quarterly* 36, no. 4 (1999): 853–68.
46 Uncredited notes to *James Joyce / Finnegans Wake* (LP: Caedmon TC 1086, 1959).
47 Marc Shell, *Stutter* (Cambridge, MA: Harvard University Press, 2005), 40. See also Steven Connor's chapter 'St … st … st' in his *Beyond Words: Sobs, Hums, Stutters and other Vocalizations* (London: Reaktion, 2014), 17–32, and Richard Elliott, '"My Tongue Gets t-t-t-": Words, Sense and Vocal Presence in Van Morrison's *It's Too Late to Stop Now*'. *Twentieth-Century Music* 13, no. 1 (2016): 53–76.
48 Other engaging audio adaptations include the epic *Waywords and Meansigns: Recreating Finnegans Wake [in its whole wholume]*, an international collaboration that has recorded the entirety of Joyce's text with original music and experimental sound art. See http://www.waywordsandmeansigns.com/.
49 A 1958 performance of 'The Wonderful Widow of Eighteen Springs' features on *The 25-Year Retrospective Concert of the Music of John Cage* (CD: Wergo WER6247-2, 1994); as noted in Chapter 4, the piece has also been recorded by Robert Wyatt on Jan Steele and John Cage, *Voices and Instruments* (LP: Obscure/Island, Obscure

No. 5, 1976). Partch's 'Isobel' and 'Annah the Allmaziful' can be heard on *Enclosure Two: Harry Partch* (CD: Innova 401, 1995). Berio's 'Omaggio a Joyce' can be heard on *An Anthology of Noise & Electronic Music: Seventh and Last A-Chronology 1930-2012* (CD: Sub Rosa SR300, 2013).

50 André Hodeir, *Anna Livia Plurabelle: A Jazz Cantata* (LP: Philips PHS 900-255, 1966). For musical references in Joyce, see Zack Bowen, *Musical Allusions in Joyce: Early Poetry through Ulysses* (Albany: State University of New York Press, 1975) and Ruth H. Bauerle, ed., *Picking Up Airs: Hearing the Music in Joyce's Text* (Urbana: University of Illinois Press, 1993). For a critical account of Hodeir's Joyce adaptation, see Tom Perchard, *After Django: Making Jazz in Postwar France* (Ann Arbor: University of Michigan Press, 2015), 105–9. Despite the ground-breaking nature of the source material, Perchard finds Hodeir's piece 'passé by the standards of both jazz and Western art music' (108).

51 Kate Bush, 'Flower of the Mountain', *Director's Cut* (CD: Fish People FPCD001, 2011); DJ Spooky That Subliminal Kid, *Rhythm Science: Excerpts and Allegories From The Sub Rosa Archives* (CD: Sub Rosa SR 201, 2004); Crystal Castles, 'Air War', *Crystal Castles* (CD: Different DIFB 1200, 2008).

Chapter 3

1 Noel Malcolm, *The Origins of English Nonsense* (London: Fontana, 1998), 14–15.

2 Brandon LaBelle, *Lexicon of the Mouth: Poetics and Politics of Voice and the Oral Imaginary* (New York: Bloomsbury, 2014), 62–3.

3 Jaap Blonk, 'A Brief History of Sound Poetry', talk given at Leamington LAMP (27 April 2013). Video available at https://www.youtube.com/watch?v=ogQk1Ym11Bc.

4 Steve McCaffery, 'Sound Poetry: A Survey', in *Sound Poetry: A Catalogue*, ed. Steve McCaffery and bpNichol (Toronto: Underwhich Editions, 1978), 6–18.

5 Roman Jakobson, *My Futurist Years*, ed. Bengt Jangfeldt and Stephen Rudy, trans. Stephen Rudy (New York: Marsilio, 1997), 177.

6 Alexei Kruchenykh, quoted in Jakobson, *My Futurist Years*, 177.

7 Nancy Perloff, 'Sound Poetry and the Musical Avant-Garde: A Musicologist's Perspective', in *The Sound of Poetry / The Poetry*

of Sound, ed. Marjorie Perloff and Craig Dworkin (Chicago: The University of Chicago Press, 2009), 101. A recording of 'Incantation by Laughter' read by Roman Jakobson, as well as work by Kruchenykh and other Russian Futurists, can be heard on *Baku: Symphony of Sirens: Sound Experiments in the Russian Avant Garde* (CD: ReR Megacorp RER RAG 1&2, 2008). For more audio and video, see the *zaum* resources archived on the PennSound website, http://writing.upenn.edu/pennsound/x/Explodity.php. For a well-produced survey of Russian Futurist book art, see Nancy Perloff, *Explodity: Sound, Image, and Word in Russian Futurist Book Art* (Los Angeles: The Getty Research Institute, 2016).

8 Velimir Khlebnikov, *Snake Train: Poetry and Prose*, trans. and ed. Gary Kern (Ann Arbor: Ardis, 1976), 62–3; Velimir Khlebnikov, *Collected Works Volume III: Selected Poems*, trans. Paul Schmidt, ed. Ronald Vroon (Cambridge, MA: Harvard University Press, 1997), 30.

9 Marnie Parsons, *Touch Monkeys: Nonsense Strategies for Reading Twentieth-Century Poetry* (Toronto: University of Toronto Press, 1994), 156.

10 Gerald Janecek, *Zaum: The Transrational Poetry of Russian Futurism* (San Diego: San Diego State University Press, 1996), 1. Paul Schmidt explains 'beyonsense' in several collections of Khlebnikov's work which he has translated; see, in particular, Velimir Khlebnikov, *Collected Works Volume I: Letters and Theoretical Writings*, trans. Paul Schmidt, ed. Charlotte Douglas (Cambridge, MA: Harvard University Press, 1987).

11 Janecek, *Zaum*, 1.

12 Khlebnikov *Collected Works Volume I*, 383.

13 Susan Stewart, *Nonsense: Aspects of Intertextuality in Folklore and Literature* (Baltimore: The Johns Hopkins University Press, 1989), 92.

14 Hugo Ball, *Flight Out of Time: A Dada Diary*, trans. Ann Raimes, ed. John Elderfield (Berkeley: University of California Press, 1996), 71. See also *The Dada Almanac*, trans. Malcolm Green et al., ed. Richard Huelsenbeck, second edn (London: Atlas, 1998); Steve McCaffery, 'Cacophony, Abstraction, and Potentiality: The Fate of the Dada Sound Poem', in *The Sound of Poetry / The Poetry of Sound*, ed. Marjorie Perloff and Craig Dworkin (Chicago: The University of Chicago Press, 2009), 118–28.

15 Ball, *Flight Out of Time*, 70–1.

16 Schwitters's three-minute recording of a section of *Ursonate*, along with his reading of his poem 'An Anna Blume', and Ernst Schwitter's 40-minute recitation of *Ursonate*, were released in the UK on a

limited edition LP in 1958 (no label or catalogue no.). Christopher Butterfield's version of the full work is on his *Music For Klein And Beuys / Ursonate / Pillar Of Snails* (CD: Artifact ART 015, 1993). Two versions by Jaap Blonk – one from 1986, another from 2003 – can be found on Kurt Schwitters and Jaap Blonk, *Ursonate* (CD: Basta 3091452, 2004). Other recitations by Blonk can be found online, as can Christian Bök's high-speed versions.

17 Henri Chopin, 'The New Media' (April 1995), trans. Sandeep Bhagwati, UbuWeb, http://www.ubu.com/sound/chopin.html (accessed 12 March 2017). The same resource also contains an interview with Chopin and his family (conducted at their home in Essex) in which Chopin discusses using the tape recorder to breaking down language into 'microparticles'.

18 Henri Chopin, 'Rouge', *Audiopoems* (CD: ? Records 05, 2001).

19 Henri Chopin, 'Le Corps', on *OU Sound Poetry: An Anthology* (LP: Alga Marghen plana-OU 15VocSon045, 2002). The longer 'Le Corpsbis' is on Henri Chopin, *Le Corpsbis & Co* (CD: Nepless PS 961 1001, 1996). For a discussion of this poem, see Cédric Jamet, 'Limitless Voice(s), Intensive Bodies: Henri Chopin's Poetics of Expansion', *Mosaic* 42, no. 2 (2009): 135–51.

20 Bob Cobbing, *ABC in Sound (Sound Poems)* (Guildford: Veer, 2015).

21 Cobbing, *ABC in Sound*, n.p.

22 The first version can be heard on Bob Cobbing, *The Spoken Word* (CD, British Library, NSACD 42, 2009). The Radiophonic Workshop version is unavailable at the time of writing; a page on Martin Guy's 'WikiDelia' website details its whereabouts: http://wikidelia.net/wiki/An_ABC_in_Sound (accessed 9 March 2017).

23 Bob Cobbing, 'Some Statements on Sound Poetry', in *Sound Poetry: A Catalogue*, ed. Steve McCaffery and bpNichol (Toronto: Underwhich Editions, 1978), 40. Reprinted in *Boooook: The Life and Work of Bob Cobbing*, ed. William Cobbing and Rosie Cooper (London: Occasional Papers, 2015), 184–5.

24 LaBelle, *Lexicon of the Mouth*, 65.

25 Ralph Stanley, 'O Death', *Music from the Motion Picture O Brother, Where Art Thou?* (CD: Mercury 170069-2, 2000); Tim Eriksen, 'O Death', *Northern Roots Live in Náměšť* (CD: Indies Scope MAM451-2, 2009); Diamanda Galás, 'O Death', *Guilty Guilty Guilty* (CD: Mute CDSTUMM274, 2008).

26 Various Artists, *Carnivocal: A Celebration of Sound Poetry* (CD: Red Deer Press / Omikron Publishing, 1999).

27 Braaxtaal, 'Muzikaret', *Speechlos* (CD: Kontrans 244, 1997). For more on Blonk, see Paul Dutton, 'Jaap Speak & Blonk Jazz', *Coda*, no. 303 (May/June 2002): 12–15.

28 See Steven Connor, *Beyond Words: Sobs, Hums, Stutters and other Vocalizations* (London: Reaktion, 2014).

29 Nicolas Collins, liner notes to Alvin Lucier, *I Am Sitting in a Room* (CD: Lovely Music LCD 1013, 1990). The quoted section of Lucier's text is also printed in these notes, but more importantly, the piece itself can be heard on the CD in a 1980 recording. The tape editor on this recording was Bob Bielecki, who also worked with Laurie Anderson on her landmark collection *United States Live* (LP: Warner Bros. 925192-1, 1984), as well as recordings released on John Giorno's Giorno Poetry Systems label. Lucier's recording is also notable as an example of the use of 'aesthetic stutter', discussed in the previous chapter.

30 Henri Chopin, liner notes to *Le Corpsbis & Co* (CD: Nepless PS 961 1001, 1996), trans. Sandeep Bhagwati.

31 Cobbing, 'Some Statements', 39.

32 Paul Lansky, liner notes to *More Than Idle Chatter* (CD: Bridge BCD9050, 1994).

33 Luciano Berio, liner notes to *Sinfonia* (LP: CBS S 34-61079, 1968).

34 Karlheinz Stockhausen, liner notes to *Hymnen* (LP: Deutsche Grammophon 2707039, 1969), trans. Gregory Biss and Rolf Gehlhaar.

35 Jean-Jacques Lecercle, *Philosophy of Nonsense: The Intuitions of Victorian Nonsense Literature* (London: Routledge, 1994), 29.

36 On Cobbing, *The Spoken Word*.

37 Malcolm Green, *The Dada Almanac*, 61.

38 Rotella's phonetic poetry can be heard on *OU Sound Poetry: An Anthology*.

39 Jandl's surface translation is included in *Verbi Visi Voco: A Performance of Poetry*, ed. Bob Cobbing, Bill Griffiths and Jennifer Pike (London: Writers Forum, 1992), 64.

40 Lecercle, *Philosophy of Nonsense*, 31.

41 *Vocology #02: 'Dada Data Wrecking Ball'*, by TTS engines reading Hugo Ball, ed. Martyn Schmidt (Digital streaming/download: Atemwerft AW 003/d, 2015), https://atemwerft.bandcamp.com/album/vocology-02-dada-data-wrecking-ball.

42 Examples include the computer Hal singing 'Daisy Bell' in *2001: A Space Odyssey*; the 'hubots' or 'synths' which are frequently breaking down in the Swedish TV series *Äkta Människor* and its English-language version *Humans*; the vari-speed robot voices in the Beastie Boys' 'Intergalactic'.

43 James Rother, 'Modernism and the Nonsense Style', *Contemporary Literature* 15, no. 2 (Spring 1974): 189.

44 Brion Gysin, *Back in No Time: The Brion Gysin Reader*, ed. Jason Weiss (Middletown: Wesleyan University Press, 2001), 93.

45 Gysin can be heard reading a suite of permutation poems on William S. Burroughs and Brion Gysin, *The Spoken Word* (CD: The British Library, NSACD 111, 2012), including the audio-manipulated 'I Am That I Am'; the collection also includes Gysin's 'Cut-Ups Self-Explained' and 'Pistol Poem', which was produced for a BBC Radio broadcast by Douglas Cleverdon (the man behind the *Alice in Wonderland* broadcast discussed in Chapter 2). Three of the permutation poems are included with musical accompaniment on Steve Lacy and Brion Gysin, *Songs* (CD: Hat Hut Hatology 625, 2006); funkier arrangements of some of them can be found on the full band arrangements by Ramuntcho Matta on Brion Gysin, *Self-Portrait Jumping* (CD: Made to Measure MTM 33, 1993.

46 There's a recording of this on the Birdyak album *Aberration* (LP: Klinker Zoundz KL8801, 1988) with added instrumental noises from Hugh Metcalfe and Ma-Lou Bangerter.

47 Cobbing, *Boooook*, 81.

48 Cobbing and Griffiths, *Verbi Visi Voco*; James Joyce, *Finnegans Wake* (London: Penguin, 2000), 341.

49 William Burroughs, 'The Cut-Up Method of Brion Gysin', *Re/Search*, no. 4/5 (1982): 36. See also *Word Virus: The William Burroughs Reader*, ed. James Grauerholz and Ira Silverberg (London: Flamingo, 1999).

50 William S. Burroughs, *Break Through in Grey Room* (LP: Sub Rosa SRV08, 2013); Burroughs and Gysin, *The Spoken Word*.

51 Jason Weiss, notes in Gysin, *Back in No Time*, 69, 79. See also Terry Wilson, 'Brion Gysin', *Re/Search*, no. 4/5 (1982): 39–43.

52 Milan Knížák, *Broken Music* (LP: Sub Rosa SR400, 2015); Milan Knížák, *Broken / Re/broken* (CD: Sub Rosa SR 409CD, 2015). On (and by) Marclay, see *On & By Christian Marclay*, ed. Jean-Pierre, Criqui (London: Whitechapel Gallery, 2014). The broken text in

relation to sound art is explored in Caleb Kelly's *Cracked Media: The Sound of Malfunction* (Cambridge, MA: MIT Press, 2009).

53 Christian Marclay, *More Encores* (CD: ReR Megacorp ReR CM1, 1997); Michel Poizat, *The Angel's Cry: Beyond the Pleasure Principle in Opera*, trans. Arthur Denner (Ithaca: Cornell University Press, 1992), 180.

54 Deborah Artman, liner notes to Bang On A Can, Concerto Köln, Rias-Kammerchor and DJ Spooky, *Lost Objects* (CD: Teldec New Line 8573-84102-2, 2001).

55 Oswald should also be heard as working in a lineage of composers working with *musique concrète* and electronic music. Richard Trythall, for example, provides a link between 1950s electroacoustic experimentation and plunderphonics; his 'Omaggio to Jerry Lee Lewis' (available on *Players And Tape* (LP: American Contemporary CRI SD 382, 1977)), does for Lewis what Berio did for Joyce, and Oswald for his plundered pop singers.

56 The lengthy liner notes to John Oswald, *69/96* (CD: Seeland SEELAND 515, 2001) provide useful insight into Oswald's sources and methods. See also Paul Hegarty, *Noise / Music: A History* (New York: Bloomsbury, 2007), 181–93, and Andrew Jones, *Plunderphonics, 'Pataphysics and Pop Mechanics: An Introduction to Musique Actuelle* (Wembley: SAF, 1995), 131–42.

57 Carl Wilson, liner notes to John Oswald, *prePlexure* (LP: Fony 82, 2014). The CD version of Plexure contains a transcription of the sounds heard as a result of the mix: John Oswald, *Plexure* (CD: Disk Union AVAN 016, 1993).

58 Robert Hunter quoted in liner notes to John Oswald, *Grayfolded* (CD: Swell/Snapper SMDCD 215, 1999).

59 On musemes and other aspects of musical meaning, see Philip Tagg, *Music's Meanings: A Modern Musicology for Non-Musos* (New York: Mass Media Music Scholars' Press, 2012). On musematic repetition, see Richard Middleton, *Studying Popular Music* (Milton Keynes: Open University Press, 1990).

60 Spoonie Gee, ' Spoonin Rap' (12-inch: Sound Of New York QC 708, 1979); A.D.O.R., 'One for the Trouble' (12-inch: Atlantic DMD 2137, 1994); Wildchild, 'Renegade Master' (12-inch: Hi Life Recordings 577131-1, 1995; Fatboy Slim's 'Old Skool Mix' is on Wildchild, 'Renegade Master 98' (12-inch: Hi Life Recordings 569 279-1, 1998). Spoonie Gee's 'One for the trouble' line – this time as used on his 1980 single 'Monster Jam' – was sampled and chopped up by Grandmaster Flash for the opening of his famous 'Adventures on the

Wheels of Steel', another track that invites reflection on remixing as narrative.

61 In addition to the remixes of Henri Chopin and James Joyce I've already mentioned, there are projects such as the Material albums *Seven Souls* (CD: Triloka/Mercury 314534905-2, 1997) and *The Road to the Western Lands* (LP: Triloka/Mercury 314558021-1, 1998). The first mixes recordings of William Burroughs with dub, while the second deconstructs and reconstructs this material further, making explicit connections to Burroughs's and Gysin's cut-ups.

62 People Like Us, aka Vicki Bennett, uses a similar plunderphonic approach to John Oswald, though often using slightly longer samples than Oswald's miniscule fragments; hear, for example, People Like Us, *Abridged Too Far* (LP: Discrepant CREP41, 2017), originally released online as digital files. The Avalanches is an Australian electronic music group that creates new pieces of music by sampling thousands of old recordings. Their 2000 debut album was reissued in 2016, along with its follow-up: *Since I Left You* (LP: XL XLLP 138, 2016); *Wildflower* (LP: Modular / XL XLLP755, 2016). Den Sorte Skole is a collective of Norwegian DJs and producers who sample thousands of records from all over the world to create new pieces of music, aiming to minimize the 'joins' between samples Hear *III* (LP: No label or cat. no., 2013) and *Indians & Cowboys* (LP: No label or cat. no., 2015). As one moves from Oswald through these examples, one is aware of an ever less fragmented soundscape, the narrative flow created by the newly combined sounds melding more smoothly into a more conventionally understood musical narrative.

Chapter 4

1 John Giorno, quoted in Marcus Boon, 'Tongue Dipped in Wisdom: John Giorno', *BOMB*, no. 105 (Fall 2008): 34.

2 Jacques Roubaud, 'Prelude: Poetry and Orality', trans. Jean-Jacques Poucel, in *The Sound of Poetry / The Poetry of Sound*, ed. Marjorie Perloff and Craig Dworkin (Chicago: The University of Chicago Press, 2009), 25.

3 'The Nobel Prize in Literature 2016: Prize Announcement', Nobelprize.org, Nobel Media AB 2014, http://www.nobelprize.org/nobel_prizes/literature/laureates/2016/announcement.html (accessed 30 March 2017).

4 Howard S. Becker, *Art Worlds* (Berkeley: University of California Press, 1982).

5 I've borrowed this term from Dewey Redman's *The Ear of the Behearer* (LP: Impulse! AS-9250, 1973), an album described by rock critic Robert Christgau as 'noise aspiring to be music' (http://www.robertchristgau.com/xg/cg/crm7406.php), which may be yet another definition of nonsense, at least that usage of 'nonsense' as a term of critique. Personally, I hold Redman's work in higher esteem than does Christgau.

6 For more on the novelty foxtrot, see and hear *Songs the Bonzo Dog Band Taught Us* (LP: Flashback FB2LP1006, 2016); the collection features several of the original 1920s and 1930s songs which the Bonzos revived.

7 The Bonzo Dog Doo-Band, 'Canyons of Your Mind', *History of the Bonzos* (LP: United Artists UAD 60071/72, 1974).

8 Bonzo Dog Band, 'My Pink Half of the Drainpipe', *History of the Bonzos*. Note that the name of the group changed slightly on different recordings.

9 Vivian Stanshall and the Sean Head Showband, 'Labio Dental Fricative', *History of the Bonzos*.

10 Although I have referred to Cutler on a few occasions in this book, his work deserves far more attention than I've given it. In addition to the earlier cited *Ludo*, his unique nonsense can be found on *Dandruff* (LP: Virgin OVED 33, 1974), *Velvet Donkey* (LP: Virgin OVED 34, 1975) and *Jammy Smears* (LP: Virgin OVED 12, 1976).

11 Stephen Fry, on *Vivian Stanshall: The Canyons of His Mind* (BBC Four broadcast, 11 June 2004).

12 Jonathan Lethem, *Talking Heads' Fear of Music* (New York: Bloomsbury Academic, 2014), 2. Talking Heads, 'I Zimbra', *Fear of Music* (LP. Sire 56707, 1979).

13 Regarding Ebbinghaus, it is instructive to read the chapter 'The Great Lalulā' in Friedrich A. Kittler, *Discourse Networks 1800 / 1900*, trans. Michael Metteer and Chris Cullens (Stanford: Stanford University Press, 1990), 206–64, which relates Ebbinghaus's work on memory and language acquisition to the nonsense poetry of Christian Morgenstern and sound recording technology. For nonsense syllables as mnemonics in music, see David W. Hughes, 'No Nonsense: The Logic and Power of Acoustic-Iconic Mnemonic Systems', *British Journal of Ethnomusicology* 9, no. 2 (2000): 93–120. My thanks to Simon McKerrell for this reference.

14 Chumbawamba, 'Ratatatay', *ABCDEFG* (CD: No Masters / Westpark NMCD33 / WP87186, 2010).

15 Clips of Dylan press conferences can be easily found online and also feature in the many documentaries that have been made about him; *Dont Look Back* (dir. D. A. Pennebaker, 1967). *Dylan on Dylan: The Essential Interviews*, ed. Jonathan Cott (London: Hodder & Stoughton, 2006), provides many typical examples of getting-it and not.

16 Marnie Parsons, *Touch Monkeys: Nonsense Strategies for Reading Twentieth-Century Poetry* (Toronto: University of Toronto Press, 1994), 17.

17 Bob Dylan, 'Ballad of a Thin Man', *Highway 61 Revisited* (LP: Columbia CL 2389, 1965). 'Ballad of a Thin Man' is included in *The Chatto Book of Nonsense* along with other Dylan songs, 'Tiny Montgomery' and 'Don't Ya Tell Henry', that draw more explicitly on nonsense terms drawn from older American vernacular music. 'Tiny Montgomery' contains the line 'do that bird', which connects Dylan to the Rivingtons and others.

18 Ed Vulliamy, 'Was 66 Pop's Greatest Year?', *The Observer Music* supplement (31 January 2016): 21.

19 The quoted lyrics come from, respectively, 'Tombstone Blues' (*Highway 61 Revisited*), 'Desolation Row' (*Highway 61 Revisited*), 'Stuck Inside of Mobile with the Memphis Blues Again', *Blonde on Blonde* (LP: Columbia CS 9316/9317, 1966) and 'Bob Dylan's 115th Dream', *Bringing It All Back Home* (LP: Columbia CS 9128, 1965). Jean-Jacques Lecercle, *Philosophy of Nonsense: The Intuitions of Victorian Nonsense Literature* (London: Routledge, 1994), 119.

20 Joseph Campbell and Henry Morton Robinson, *A Skeleton Key to Finnegans Wake: Unlocking James Joyce's Masterwork*, ed. Edmund L. Epstein (Novato: New World Library, 2013), 3.

21 Terence McKenna, 'Surfing on Finnegans Wake', lecture delivered at Esalen Institute, Big Sur in 1995. The lecture was uploaded to YouTube on 12 April 2015 (https://www.youtube.com/watch?v=0QrWfbYFtNk), and has been transcribed at https://terencemckenna.wikispaces.com/Surfing+on+Finnegans+Wake. McKenna makes an additional musical comparison that is worth noting in the context of this book; 'the great technique of the 20th century is collage or pastiche. It was originally developed by the Dadaists in Zurich in 1919. Right now it's having a huge resurgence in the form of sampling in pop music and Joyce was the supreme sampler.'

22 'Weird Al' Yankovic, 'Bob', *The Essential* (CD: Way Moby / Volcano / Legacy, 2009). This collection also contains Yankovic's 'Smells like Nirvana', which plays on the famous incomprehensibility of Kurt Cobain's lyrics and 'The Saga Begins', a parody of Don McLean's 'American Pie' that re-tells the plot of *Star Wars*. McLean's song has enjoyed a reputation as a riddle to be solved ever since its release in 1971. In 2015, it was reported that the singer-songwriter had 'finally revealed the meaning behind ... one of the most enigmatic songs in pop history'. Rob Crilly, 'Don McLean reveals secrets behind American Pie', *The Telegraph* online edition (7 April 2015), http://www.telegraph.co.uk/news/worldnews/northamerica/usa/11518734/Don-McLean-reveals-secrets-behind-American-Pie.html. See also Susan Stewart's discussion of palindromes in *Nonsense*, 70–1.

23 Robert Wyatt, 'Blues in Bob Minor', *Shleep* (LP: Domino REWIGLP45, 2008).

24 Parsons, *Touch Monkeys*, 151.

25 See *Boooook: The Life and Work of Bob Cobbing*, ed. William Cobbing and Rosie Cooper (London: Occasional Papers, 2015); *The Alphabet Game: A bpNichol Reader*, ed. Darren Wershler-Henry and Lori Emerson (Toronto: Coach House, 2007); bpNichol, *A Book of Variations: Love – Zygal – Art Facts* (Toronto: Coach House, 2013).

26 Robert Wyatt quoted in Barney Hoskyns, '8 out of 10 Cats Prefer Whiskers', *Mojo*, No. 64 (March 1999): 44.

27 Robert Wyatt, *Rock Bottom* (CD: Hannibal HNCD 1426, 1998).

28 Uncredited liner notes (presumably by Wyatt) to Jan Steele and John Cage, *Voices and Instruments* (LP: Obscure/Island, Obscure No. 5, 1976). The collaborations with Michael Mantler can be found on the latter's *The Hapless Child and Other Inscrutable Stories* (LP: WATT Works / Virgin WATT/4, 1976), *Silence* (LP: WATT Works / Virgin WATT/ 5, 1977) and *Hide and Seek* (CD: ECM, ECM1738, 2001)).

29 It was my fascination with Wyatt's work that led me to start considering relationships between popular music, nonsense and experimental literature in the first place, forming the seeds of this book. Extended versions of the brief discussion of Wyatt in this chapter can be found in my 'You Can't Just Say "Words"': Literature and Nonsense in the Work of Robert Wyatt', in *Litpop: Writing and Popular Music*, ed. Rachel Carroll and Adam Hansen (Farnham: Ashgate, 2014), 49–62, and '"Words Take the Place of Meaning": Sound, Sense and Politics in the Music of Robert Wyatt', in *The Singer-Songwriter in Europe: Paradigms, Politics and Place*, ed. Isabelle Marc and Stuart Green (London: Routledge, 2016), 51–64.

30 Morgan Fisher, *Miniatures One & Two* (CD: Cherry Red, CDBRED361, 2008).
31 Gilad Atzmon, *Musik: Re-Arranging the 20th Century* (CD: Enja, TIP-8888482, 2004).
32 Brandon LaBelle, *Lexicon of the Mouth: Poetics and Politics of Voice and the Oral Imaginary* (New York: Bloomsbury, 2014), 63.
33 Nadav Appel, '"Ga, ga, ooh-la-la": The Childlike Use of Language in Pop-Rock Music', *Popular Music*, 33, no. 1 (2014): 96.
34 Susan Stewart, 'Rhyme and Freedom', in *The Sound of Poetry / The Poetry of Sound*, ed. Marjorie Perloff and Craig Dworkin (Chicago: The University of Chicago Press, 2009), 43.
35 Various Artists, *Great Googa Mooga!* (CD: Ace CDCHD 880, 2003).
36 Wilson Pickett, 'Land of 1000 Dances', *The Exciting Wilson Pickett* (LP: Atlantic SD 8129, 1966). The refrain was an addition to Chris Kenner's original 1962 song; it first appeared on a 1965 version by Cannibal and the Headhunters and was subsequently adopted by Pickett. Little Richard, 'Tutti Frutti', *All-Time Hits* (LP: Specialty SNTF 5000, 1969).
37 Margaret Mahy, *Nonstop Nonsense*, ill. Quentin Blake (London: Puffin, 1977), 11.
38 Thomas Brothers, *Louis Armstrong: Master of Modernism* (New York: W. W. Norton, 2014), 211–21.
39 See Hughes, 'No Nonsense'.
40 William R. Bauer, 'Scat Singing: A Timbral and Phonemic Analysis', *Current Musicology*, nos. 71–73 (Spring 2001–Spring 2002): 303–23.
41 All tracks available on Louis Armstrong, *Hot Fives and Sevens* (CD: JSP JSPLOUISBOX 100, 1999).
42 Barry Kernfeld, *What to Listen for in Jazz* (New Haven: Yale University Press, 1997), 167.
43 Bauer, 'Scat Singing', 310. Carter's version of 'Babe's Blues' can be heard on *Out There with Betty Carter* (LP: Peacock Records PLP 90, 1958).
44 Ira Gitler, liner notes to King Pleasure and Annie Ross, *King Pleasure Sings, Annie Ross Sings* (LP: Prestige P7128, 1986).
45 Ira Steingrout, liner notes to Eddie Jefferson, *There I Go Again* (LP: Prestige P-24095, 1980).
46 The quotation from *Time* is included in the liner notes of Lambert, Hendricks & Ross, *The Hottest New Group in Jazz* (LP: Columbia CL1403, 1960). On jazz as a coded language, see Neil Leonard, 'The

Jazzman's Verbal Usage', *Black American Literature Forum* 20, no. 1/2 (1986): 151–60. Nonsense as domestic language is discussed briefly in Elliott, 'You Can't Just Say "Words"'.

47 *Slim Gaillard's Civilisation* (dir. Anthony Wall, 1989). Most of Gaillard's classic songs can be heard on *The Extrovert Spirit of Slim Gaillard* (CD: Avid AMSC1141, 2014).

48 Hughes, 'No Nonsense', 93–4.

49 Parsons, *Touch Monkeys*, 144.

50 Timothy Wise, 'Yodel Species: A Typology of Falsetto Effects in Popular Music Vocal Styles', *Radical Musicology* 2 (2007): 57 pars, http://www.radical-musicology.org.uk.

51 Butch Hancock, 'West Texas Waltz', *Own & Own* (LP: Demon D-FIEND 150, 1989).

52 All these songs can be found on Shirley Ellis, *The Complete Congress Recordings* (CD: Connoisseur Collection VSOP CD, 2001).

53 For a good overview, see the compilations *Doo Wop: The R&B Vocal Group Sound 1950-1960* (CD: Fantastic Voyage FVTD 129, 2011), *Doo Wop: The Rock & Roll Vocal Group Sound 1957-1961* (CD: Fantastic Voyage FVTD 129, 2012) and *Doo Wop Revival: The R&B Vocal Group Sound 1961-1962* (CD: Fantastic Voyage FVTD 190, 2014).

54 Bernard Gendron, 'Theodor Adorno Meets the Cadillacs', in *Studies in Entertainment: Critical Approaches to Mass Culture*, ed. Tania Modleski (Bloomington: Indiana University Press, 1986), 18–36.

55 Lawrence Pitilli, *Doo-Wop Acappella: A Story of Street Corners, Echoes, and Three-Part Harmonies* (Lanham: Rowman & Littlefield, 2016), 56.

56 Barry Mann, 'Who Put the Bomp (in the Bomp Bomp Bomp)', *Doo Wop: The Rock & Roll Vocal Group Sound*.

57 The Rivingtons, *The Liberty Years* (CD: EMI CDP-7-95204-2, 1991); Trashmen, The. *Surfin' Bird* (CD: Sundazed SC 6064, 2010).

58 Stephen Fry, 'The Joy of Gibberish', *Fry's English Delight*, Season 2, ep. 4 (Audible download, 2010). With regard to the *Not Only … But Also* sketch, the name Bo Dudley is obviously a play on Bo Diddley and it is worth noting the latter's fondness for nonsense and slang in his name and music; his first album contains such gems as 'Diddey Wah Diddey', 'Diddley Daddy' and 'Hey! Bo Diddley', the latter of which has a first line derived from the nursery rhyme 'Old MacDonald's Farm' (all tracks on Bo Diddley, *Bo Diddley* (LP: Chess LP-1431, 1958)). This 'Diddey Wah Diddey'

is different to the song recorded earlier by blues singer Blind Blake as 'Diddie Wa Diddie', which made its way into *The Chatto Book of Nonsense Poetry* and contained the line 'I wish somebody would tell me what diddie wa diddie means'. (Blind Blake, 'Diddie Wa Diddie', *Complete Recorded Works in Chronological Order, Volume 3 (May 1928 To August 1929)* (CD: Document DOCD-5026, 1991). A follow-up song finds the singer claiming he now knows what 'diddie wa diddie' means following some trouble with the law. Blind Blake, 'Diddie Wa Diddie No. 2', *Complete Recorded Works in Chronological Order, Volume 4 (August 1929 To June 1932)* (CD: Document DOCD-5027, 1991). Manfred Mann took 'Do Wah Diddy Diddy', a cover of a 1963 song by The Exciters, to the top of the UK charts in 1964. And let's not forget P. Diddy, the pseudonym adopted by rapper Sean Combs after abandoning his previous stage name Puff Daddy. In 2014 Combs resumed using the name under which he had first become famous, leading to a newspaper headline which read 'Sean Combs renounces P Diddy to become Puff Daddy again' and a story whose first sentence provides a classic example of language which only makes sense to those in the know: 'After Puffying and Diddying for almost a decade, Sean Combs is once again Puff Daddy' (*The Guardian*, online edition (14 March 2014)).

59 Leonard Cohen quoted in *Leonard Cohen on Leonard Cohen: Interviews and Encounters*, ed. Jeff Burger (Chicago: Chicago Review Press, 2014), 356. The 'great mysteries' routine can be heard on his *Live in London* (CD: Columbia 88697405022, 2009).

60 Lou Reed, 'Walk on the Wild Side', *Transformer* (LP: RCA Victor LSP-4807, 1972). The backing vocals were provided by the white British vocal trio Thunderthighs, who also had a brief recording career in which they performed lead as well as backing vocals. Their 1974 single 'Central Park Arrest' (Philips 6006 386), composed by singer-songwriter Lynsey de Paul, featured a vocal arrangement similar to that used in 'Walk on the Wild Side'.

61 Ezra Furman quoted in Kieron Tyler, 'Ezra Furman', *Mojo*, no. 263 (October 2015): 26.

62 Paul Dutton, liner notes to CD accompanying *Musicworks 54* (Autumn 1992). A recording of the piece is included on the CD.

63 Another recording of 'Beyond Doo-Dop' can be heard on Dutton's *Mouth Pieces* (CD: OHM OHM/AVTR 021, 2000), which also includes a piece entitled 'M's 'n' m's' that recalls the Rivingtons' 'Papa-Oom-Mow-Mow' with its opening section featuring rhythmically stressed lines of 'm's'.

64 Paul Dutton, 'Beyond Doo-Wop or How I Came to Realize that Hank Williams is Avant-Garde', *Musicworks*, no. 54 (Autumn 1992): 8–19 (quoted material from p. 9).

65 Christian Bök in conversation with Charles Bernstein, 'On Being Stubborn: Close Listening with Christian Bök', Studio 111, University of Pennsylvania (20 April 2005), archived at the PennSound website, http://writing.upenn.edu/pennsound/x/Bok.php (accessed 9 March 2017) and transcribed at Jacket2.org (21 April 2011), https://jacket2.org/interviews/being-stubborn (accessed 9 March 2017).

66 Nicole Paris's videos can be found via her YouTube channel (https://www.youtube.com/channel/UCSkZVT6Vupj7e9iIvROHV4Q/videos) and feature numerous jams and contests with her father Edward Cage. Paris has also collaborated with beatboxing pioneer Doug E. Fresh in a cypher for the 2015 BET Hip-Hop Awards. Eklips became famous for his routine 'The History of Hip Hop', which mixes classic beatboxing with brief fragments of vocal and other melodic lines; a version entitled 'The most amazing beat box video ever!!! 4 minutes hip hop history by Eklips for Trace', uploaded 24 January 2011, had received over 50 million views on YouTube at the time of writing (https://www.youtube.com/watch?v=g0_2vmkTmf0). A less-viewed version, uploaded 3 June 2012, overlays Eklips' performance with video footage of the hip-hop tracks being referenced (https://www.youtube.com/watch?v=dRhmsx6PdJU). Reggie Watts's imitation of rapping styles consists of nonsense language presented as actual language that can't quite be understood; numerous performances can be found online.

67 Sugarhill Gang's 'Rapper's Delight' and Busy Bee's 'Making Cash Money' can both be found on *A Complete Introduction to Sugar Hill Records* (CD: Universal / Sanctuary / Castle 2736484, 2010). The nonsense riff from Busy Bee's song resurfaces in A Tribe Called Quest's 'Rap Promoter' (1991) and Kid Rock's 'Bawitdaba' (1998), showing once more the lasting vitality of specific nonsense strands.

68 Darryl McDaniels in an interview for *Hip-Hop Evolution*, ep. 3 (dir. Darby Wheeler, Sam Dunn and Scot McFadyen, Canada, 2016).

69 Smiley Culture, 'Cockney Translation' (12-inch: Fashion Records FAD 020, 1984); Big L, 'Ebonics / Size 'Em Up' (12-inch: Flamboyant Entertainment FB-139, 1998); True Tiger feat. P Money, 'Slang Like This', released 11 October 2010, uploaded to YouTube 8 November 2010, https://www.youtube.com/watch?v=2fIrIg8pSV4; Aems, 'Geordie Slang Like This', uploaded to YouTube 7 June 2011, https://www.youtube.com/watch?v=w0ep0XcXkiU. A Serbian version by Zvezde Grajma was uploaded to YouTube 25 November

2011 (https://www.youtube.com/watch?v=Fkznx-Vd8-w) and a Croatian version by Dregermajster Crew on 11 May 2012 (https://www.youtube.com/watch?v=auUcv9-nY5o). I'm grateful to Iván Diaz Burlinson for bringing the 'Slang Like This' examples to my attention.

70 Wayne Marshall, 'Follow Me Now: The Zigzagging Zunguzung Meme', Wayne&Wax (10 May 2007, updated subsequently), http://wayneandwax.com/?p=137.

71 Kano, 'New Banger', *Made in the Manor* (LP: Parlophone 082564 6484232, 2016).

72 Christian Vander quoted in *The Wire*, no. 381 (November 2015): 36–7. For musical examples, hear Magma, *Theusz Hamtaahk – Trilogie* (CD: Seventh SRA 29-30-31, 2001).

73 Ethan Hayden, *Sigur Rós's ( )* (New York: Bloomsbury Academic, 2014); Sigur Rós. *( )* (LP: FatCat FATLP22 / [PIAS] PIASB122dlp, 2002).

74 Ken Hollings, review of Stereolab's *Sound-Dust*, *The Wire*, no. 211 (September 2001): 53.

75 Ian Penman, *Vital Signs: Music, Movies and Other Manias* (London: Serpent's Tail, 1998), 367, 368.

Conclusion

1 Unlike the other items in this list, the last quoted material has not previously been mentioned in this book. It's from Sir Thomas Urqhart's translation of Rabelais, collected in *The Chatto Book of Cabbages and Kings: Lists in Literature*, ed. Francis Spufford (London: Chatto & Windus, 1989), 79.

2 Jesse Dangerously, 'Tom Lehrer's The Elements', *How to Express Your Dissenting Political Viewpoint Through Origami* (CD: Backburner Recordings HPK0006). Jesse Dangerously has also included a recording of Carroll's 'Jabberwocky'. Tom Lehrer's original 'The Elements' (a list of the chemical elements contained in the Periodic Table) can be heard on Tom Lehrer, *More of Tom Lehrer* (LP: Decca LF 1323, 1959). Lehrer's song took its listing influence from Gershwin's 'Tchaikovsky and Other Russians' and musical influence from Gilbert and Sullivan's 'Major-General's Song'.

3 Stanley Unwin, 'The Populode of the Musicolly', *Rotatey Diskers with Unwin* (CD: Castle Pie PIESD289, 2002).

4 One starting point might be the track 'Honki Ponki', which travels from Turkey in Senay's 1980 original to Japan in a 2009 cover version by OOIOO.

5 Laurence Sterne, *The Life and Opinions of Tristram Shandy, Gentleman*, ed. Graham Petrie (Harmondsworth: Penguin, 1977), 165.

6 Jean-Jacques Lecercle, *Philosophy through the Looking-Glass: Language, Nonsense, Desire* (London: Hutchinson, 1985). Jaap Blonk does something analogous in his piece 'Bla-blaing on No Nonsense', which can be heard on Braaxtal's self-titled album (CD: CD. Kontrans 939, 1993).

7 Jean-Jacques Lecercle, *Philosophy of Nonsense: The Intuitions of Victorian Nonsense Literature* (London: Routledge, 1994), 38, 40.

BIBLIOGRAPHY

Appel, Nadav. '"Ga, ga, ooh-la-la": The Childlike Use of Language in Pop-Rock Music'. *Popular Music* 33, no. 1 (2014): 91–108.
Bakhtin, Mikhail. *Rabelais and His World*. Translated by Hélène Iswolsky. Bloomington: Indiana University Press, 1984.
Ball, Hugo. *Flight Out of Time: A Dada Diary*. Edited by John Elderfield. Translated by Ann Raimes. Berkeley: University of California Press, 1996.
Bauer, William R. 'Scat Singing: A Timbral and Phonemic Analysis'. *Current Musicology*, nos. 71–3 (Spring 2001–Spring 2002): 303–23.
Bauerle, Ruth H., ed. *Picking Up Airs: Hearing the Music in Joyce's Text*. Urbana: University of Illinois Press, 1993.
Becker, Howard S. *Art Worlds*. Berkeley: University of California Press, 1982.
Bellos, David. *Is That a Fish in Your Ear?: Translation and the Meaning of Everything*. London: Penguin, 2011.
Blonk, Jaap. 'Some words to Kurt Schwitters' URSONATE'. Jaap Blonk's Web Pages, http://www.jaapblonk.com/Texts/ursonatewords.html.
Brothers, Thomas. *Louis Armstrong: Master of Modernism*. New York: W. W. Norton, 2014.
Boon, Marcus. 'Tongue Dipped in Wisdom: John Giorno'. *BOMB*, no. 105 (Fall 2008): 30–6.
Bowen, Zack. *Musical Allusions in Joyce: Early Poetry through Ulysses*. Albany: State University of New York Press, 1975.
Burger, Jeff, ed. *Leonard Cohen on Leonard Cohen: Interviews and Encounters*. Chicago: Chicago Review Press, 2014.
Burroughs, William. 'The Cut-Up Method of Brion Gysin'. *Re/Search*, no. 4/5 (1982): 35–6.
Burroughs, William. *Word Virus: The William Burroughs Reader*. Edited by James Grauerholz and Ira Silverberg. London: Flamingo, 1999.
Campbell, Joseph and Henry Morton Robinson. *A Skeleton Key to Finnegans Wake: Unlocking James Joyce's Masterwork*. Edited by Edmund L. Epstein. Novato: New World Library, 2013.
Carroll, Lewis. *The Annotated Alice: Alice's Adventures in Wonderland & Through the Looking-Glass*. Definitive Edition. With illustrations

by John Tenniel. Updated, with an introduction and notes by Martin Gardner. New York: W. W. Norton, 2000.

Cobbing, Bob. *ABC in Sound (Sound Poems)*. Guildford: Veer, 2015.

Cobbing, Bob, Bill Griffiths and Jennifer Pike, eds. *Verbi Visi Voco: A Performance of Poetry*. London: Writers Forum, 1992.

Cobbing, William and Rosie Cooper, eds. *Boooook: The Life and Work of Bob Cobbing*. London: Occasional Papers, 2015.

Colley, Ann. 'Edwared Lear's Limericks and the Reversals of Nonsense'. *Victorian Poetry* 26, no. 3, Comic Verse (Autumn 1988): 285–99.

Connor, James A. 'Radio Free Joyce: "Wake" Language and the Experience of Radio'. *James Joyce Quarterly* 30, no. 4/31, no. 1 (1993): 825–43.

Connor, Steven. *James Joyce*. Plymouth: Northcote House, 1996.

Connor, Steven. *Beyond Words: Sobs, Hums, Stutters and other Vocalizations*. London: Reaktion, 2014.

Cott, Jonathan, ed. *Dylan on Dylan: The Essential Interviews*. London: Hodder & Stoughton, 2006.

Criqui, Jean-Pierre, ed. *On & By Christian Marclay*. London: Whitechapel Gallery, 2014.

Deleuze, Gilles. *The Logic of Sense*. Translated by Mark Lester with Charles Stival. Edited by Constantin V. Boundas. London: The Athlone Press, 1990.

Dolar, Mladen. *A Voice and Nothing More*. Cambridge, MA: The MIT Press, 2006.

Dutton, Paul. 'Beyond Doo-Wop or How I Came to Realize that Hank Williams is Avant-Garde'. *Musicworks*, no. 54 (Autumn 1992): 8–19.

Dutton, Paul. 'Jaap Speak & Blonk Jazz'. *Coda*, no. 303 (May/June 2002): 12–15.

Eco, Umberto. *Mouse or Rat?: Translation as Negotiation*. London: Weidenfeld & Nicolson, 2003.

Eliot, T. S. *On Poetry and Poets*. London: Faber and Faber, 1957.

Elliott, Richard. 'You Can't Just Say "Words"': Literature and Nonsense in the Work of Robert Wyatt'. In *Litpop: Writing and Popular Music*, edited by Rachel Carroll and Adam Hansen, 49–62. Farnham: Ashgate, 2014.

Elliott, Richard. '"Words Take the Place of Meaning": Sound, Sense and Politics in the Music of Robert Wyatt'. In *The Singer-Songwriter in Europe: Paradigms, Politics and Place*, edited by Isabelle Marc and Stuart Green, 51–64. London: Routledge, 2016.

Elliott, Richard. '"My Tongue Gets t-t-t-": Words, Sense and Vocal Presence in Van Morrison's *It's Too Late to Stop Now*'. *Twentieth-Century Music* 13, no. 1 (2016): 53–76.

Flescher, Jacqueline. 'The Language of Nonsense in *Alice*'. *Yale French Studies*, no. 43, The Child's Part (1969): 128–44.
Gendron, Bernard. 'Theodor Adorno Meets the Cadillacs'. In *Studies in Entertainment: Critical Approaches to Mass Culture*, edited by Tania Modleski, 18–36. Bloomington: Indiana University Press, 1986.
Gysin, Brion. *Back in No Time: The Brion Gysin Reader*. Edited by Jason Weiss. Middletown: Wesleyan University Press, 2001.
Haughton, Hugh, ed. *The Chatto Book of Nonsense Poetry*. London: Chatto & Windus, 1988.
Hayden, Ethan. *Sigur Rós's* ( ). New York: Bloomsbury Academic, 2014.
Hegarty, Paul. *Noise / Music: A History*. New York: Bloomsbury, 2007.
Heyman, Michael. *Isles of Boshen: Edward Lear's Literary Nonsense in Context*. PhD Dissertation. University of Glasgow, 1999. Available at dspace.gla.ac.uk.
Heyman, Michael, Sumanyu Satpathy and Anushka Ravishankar, eds. *The Tenth Rasa: An Anthology of Indian Nonsense*. New Delhi: Penguin, 2007.
Huelsenbeck, Richard, ed. *The Dada Almanac*. English edition presented by Malcolm Green, additional matter edited by Malcolm Green and Alastair Brotchie. Translated by Malcolm Green et al. Second edition. London: Atlas, 1998.
Hughes, David W. 'No Nonsense: The Logic and Power of Acoustic-Iconic Mnemonic Systems'. *British Journal of Ethnomusicology* 9, no. 2 (2000): 93–120.
Ihde, Don. *Listening and Voice: Phenomenologies of Sound*. Second edition. Albany: State University of New York Press, 2007.
Jakobson, Roman. *My Futurist Years*. Compiled and edited by Bengt Jangfeldt and Stephen Rudy. Translated by Stephen Rudy. New York: Marsilio, 1997.
Jamet, Cédric. 'Limitless Voice(s), Intensive Bodies: Henri Chopin's Poetics of Expansion'. *Mosaic* 42, no. 2 (2009): 135–51.
Janecek, Gerald. *Zaum: The Transrational Poetry of Russian Futurism*. San Diego: San Diego State University Press, 1996.
Jones, Andrew. *Plunderphonics, 'Pataphysics and Pop Mechanics: An Introduction to* Musique Actuelle. Wembley: SAF, 1995.
Joyce, James. *Ulysses: The 1922 Text*. Edited by Jeri Johnson. Oxford: Oxford University Press, 1998.
Joyce, James. *Finnegans Wake*. London: Penguin, 2000.
Kahn, Douglas. *Noise, Water, Meat: A History of Sound in the Arts*. Cambridge, MA: MIT Press, 1999.
Kelly, Caleb. *Cracked Media: The Sound of Malfunction*. Cambridge, MA: MIT Press, 2009.

Kenner, Hugh. *Joyce's Voices*. Berkeley: University of California Press, 1978.
Kernfeld, Barry. *What to Listen for in Jazz*. New Haven: Yale University Press, 1997.
Kershner, R. Brandon. *Joyce, Bakhtin, and Popular Literature: Chronicles of Disorder*. Chapel Hill: The University of North Carolina Press, 1989.
Khlebnikov, Velimir. *Collected Works Volume I: Letters and Theoretical Writings*. Translated by Paul Schmidt. Edited by Charlotte Douglas. Cambridge, MA: Harvard University Press, 1987.
Khlebnikov, Velimir. *Collected Works Volume III: Selected Poems*. Translated by Paul Schmidt. Edited by Ronald Vroon. Cambridge, MA: Harvard University Press, 1997.
Khlebnikov, Velimir. *Snake Train: Poetry and Prose*. Edited by Gary Kern. Translated by Gary Kern, Richard Sheldon, Edward J. Brown, Neil Cornwell and Lily Feiler. Ann Arbor: Ardis, 1976.
Kittler, Friedrich A. *Discourse Networks 1800 / 1900*. Translated by Michael Metteer and Chris Cullens. Stanford: Stanford University Press, 1990.
LaBelle, Brandon. *Lexicon of the Mouth: Poetics and Politics of Voice and the Oral Imaginary*. New York: Bloomsbury, 2014.
Lear, Edward. *The Complete Nonsense and Other Verse*. Edited by Vivien Noakes. London: Penguin, 2006.
Lecercle, Jean-Jacques. *Philosophy of Nonsense: The Intuitions of Victorian Nonsense Literature*. London: Routledge, 1994.
Lecercle, Jean-Jacques. *Philosophy through the Looking-Glass: Language, Nonsense, Desire*. London: Hutchinson, 1985.
Leonard, Neil. 'The Jazzman's Verbal Usage'. *Black American Literature Forum* 20, no. 1/2 (1986): 151–60.
Lethem, Jonathan. *Talking Heads' Fear of Music*. New York: Bloomsbury Academic, 2014.
Mahy, Margaret. *Nonstop Nonsense*. Illustrated by Quentin Blake. London: Puffin, 1977.
Malcolm, Noel. *The Origins of English Nonsense*. London: Fontana, 1998.
Marshall, Wayne. 'Follow Me Now: The Zigzagging Zunguzung Meme'. Wayne&Wax (10 May 2007, updated subsequently), http://wayneandwax.com/?p=137.
McCaffery, Steve. 'Sound Poetry: A Survey'. In *Sound Poetry: A Catalogue*, edited by Steve McCaffery and bp Nichol, 6–18. Toronto: Underwhich Editions, 1978.
McCaffery, Steve. 'Cacophony, Abstraction, and Potentiality: The Fate of the Dada Sound Poem'. In *The Sound of Poetry / The Poetry of Sound*,

edited by Marjorie Perloff and Craig Dworkin, 118–28. Chicago: The University of Chicago Press, 2009.
McCaffery, Steve and bp Nichol, eds. *Sound Poetry: A Catalogue*. Toronto: Underwhich Editions, 1978.
Middleton, Richard. *Studying Popular Music*. Milton Keynes: Open University Press, 1990.
Nancy, Jean-Luc. *Listening*. Translated by Charlotte Mandell. New York: Fordham University Press, 2007.
Nichol, bp. *A Book of Variations: Love – Zygal – Art Facts*. Toronto: Coach House, 2013.
Nichol, bp. *The Alphabet Game: A bpNichol Reader*. Edited by Darren Wershler-Henry and Lori Emerson. Toronto: Coach House, 2007.
Parsons, Marnie. *Touch Monkeys: Nonsense Strategies for Reading Twentieth-Century Poetry*. Toronto: University of Toronto Press, 1994.
Peake, Mervyn. *Complete Nonsense*. Edited by Robert W. Maslan and G. Peter Winnington. Manchester: Carcanet, 2011.
Penman, Ian. *Vital Signs: Music, Movies and Other Manias*. London: Serpent's Tail, 1998.
Perchard, Tom. *After Django: Making Jazz in Postwar France*. Ann Arbor: University of Michigan Press, 2015.
Perloff, Marjorie and Craig Dworkin, eds. *The Sound of Poetry / The Poetry of Sound*. Chicago: The University of Chicago Press, 2009.
Perloff, Nancy. *Explodity: Sound, Image, and Word in Russian Futurist Book Art*. Los Angeles: The Getty Research Institute, 2016.
Perloff, Nancy. 'Sound Poetry and the Musical Avant-Garde: A Musicologist's Perspective'. In *The Sound of Poetry / The Poetry of Sound*, edited by Marjorie Perloff and Craig Dworkin, 97–117. Chicago: The University of Chicago Press, 2009.
Piette, Adam. *Remembering and the Sound of Words: Mallarmé, Proust, Joyce, Beckett*. Oxford: Clarendon Press, 1996.
Pitilli, Lawrence. *Doo-Wop Acappella: A Story of Street Corners, Echoes, and Three-Part Harmonies*. Lanham: Rowman & Littlefield, 2016.
Poizat, Michel. *The Angel's Cry: Beyond the Pleasure Principle in Opera*. Translated by Arthur Denner. Ithaca: Cornell University Press, 1992.
Rabelais, François. *Gargantua*. Translated by Andrew Brown. London: 100 Pages, 2003.
Ríos, Julián. *The House of Ulysses*. Translated by Nick Caistor. Champaign: Dalkey Archive, 2010.
Ríos, Julián. *Larva: Midsummer Night's Babel*. Translated by Richard Alan Francis, Suzanne Jill Levine and Julián Ríos. London: Dalkey Archive, 2004.
Rother, James. 'Modernism and the Nonsense Style'. *Contemporary Literature* 15, no. 2 (Spring 1974): 187–202.

Roubaud, Jacques. 'Prelude: Poetry and Orality'. Translated by Jean-Jacques Poucel. In *The Sound of Poetry / The Poetry of Sound*, edited by Marjorie Perloff and Craig Dworkin, 18–25. Chicago: The University of Chicago Press, 2009.

Rubery, Matthew. *Audiobooks, Literature, and Sound Studies*. New York: Routledge, 2011.

Schwarz, David. *Listening Subjects: Music, Psychoanalysis, Culture*. Durham, NC: Duke University Press, 1997.

Sewell, Elizabeth. *The Field of Nonsense*. London: Chatto and Windus, 1952.

Shaw Sailer, Susan. 'Universalizing Languages: *Finnegans Wake* Meets Basic English'. *James Joyce Quarterly* 36, no. 4 (1999): 853–68.

Shell, Marc. *Stutter*. Cambridge, MA: Harvard University Press, 2005.

Shockley, Alan. *Music in the Words: Musical Form and Counterpoint in the Twentieth-Century Novel*. Farnham: Ashgate, 2009.

Spufford, Francis, ed. *The Chatto Book of Cabbages and Kings: Lists in Literature*. London: Chatto & Windus, 1989.

Stein, Gertrude. *Tender Buttons*. The Corrected Centennial Edition. Edited by Seth Perlow. San Francisco: City Lights, 2014.

Sterne, Laurence. *The Life and Opinions of Tristram Shandy, Gentleman*. Edited by Graham Petrie. Harmondsworth: Penguin, 1977.

Stewart, Susan. *Nonsense: Aspects of Intertextuality in Folklore and Literature*. Baltimore: The Johns Hopkins University Press, 1989.

Stewart, Susan. 'Rhyme and Freedom'. In *The Sound of Poetry / The Poetry of Sound*, edited by Marjorie Perloff and Craig Dworkin, 29–48. Chicago: The University of Chicago Press, 2009.

Tagg, Philip. *Music's Meanings: A Modern Musicology for Non-Musos*. New York: Mass Media Music Scholar's Press, 2012.

Tarantino, Elisabetta and Carlo Caruso, eds. *Nonsense and Other Senses: Regulated Absurdity in Literature*. Newcastle upon Tyne: Cambridge Scholars, 2009.

Thwaite, Mark. 'Interview with Julián Ríos'. *Context*, no. 17 (n.d.). Dalkey Archive Press website, http://www.dalkeyarchive.com/interview-with-julian-rios.

Tigges, Wim. *An Anatomy of Literary Nonsense*. Amsterdam: Rodopi: 1988.

Tigges, Wim, ed. *Explorations in the Field of Nonsense*. Amsterdam: Rodopi: 1987.

Wilson, Terry. 'Brion Gysin'. *Re/Search*, no. 4/5 (1982): 39–43.

Wise, Timothy. 'Yodel Species: A Typology of Falsetto Effects in Popular Music Vocal Styles'. *Radical Musicology* 2 (2007): 57pars, http://www.radical-musicology.org.uk.

DISCOGRAPHY

A.D.O.R. 'One for the Trouble'. 12-inch. Atlantic DMD 2137, 1994.
Alice in Wonderland. Adapted and produced by Douglas Cleverdon. LP. Argo. ZTA 501-2, 1958.
Anderson, Laurie. *United States Live*. LP. Warner Bros. 925192-1, 1984.
Armstrong, Louis. *Hot Fives and Sevens*. CD. JSP JSPLOUISBOX 100, 1999.
Atzmon, Gilad. *Musik: Re-Arranging the 20th Century*. CD. Enja, TIP-8888482, 2004.
Avalanches, The. *Since I Left You*. LP: XL XLLP 138, 2016.
Avalanches, The. *Wildflower*. LP: Modular / XL XLLP755, 2016.
Ball, Patrick. *Finnegans Wake*. CD. Celestial Harmonies 14113-2, 1997.
Bang On A Can, Concerto Köln, Rias-Kammerchor and DJ Spooky. *Lost Objects*. CD. Teldec New Line 8573-84102-2, 2001.
Berio, Luciano. *Sinfonia*. LP. CBS S 34-61079, 1968.
Big L. 'Ebonics / Size 'Em Up'. 12-inch single. Flamboyant Entertainment FB-139, 1998.
Birdyak. *Aberration*. LP. Klinker Zoundz KL8801, 1988.
Blind Blake. *Complete Recorded Works in Chronological Order, Volume 3 (May 1928 To August 1929)*. CD. Document DOCD-5026, 1991.
Blind Blake. *Complete Recorded Works in Chronological Order, Volume 4 (August 1929 To June 1932)*. CD (Document DOCD-5027, 1991.
Bonzo Dog Band, The. *History of the Bonzos*. LP. United Artists UAD 60071/72, 1974.
Braaxtaal. *Braaxtaal*. CD. Kontrans 939, 1993.
Braaxtaal. *Speechlos*. CD. Kontrans 244, 1997.
Burroughs, William S. *Break Through in Grey Room*. LP. Sub Rosa SRV08, 2013.
Burroughs, William S. and Brion Gysin. *The Spoken Word*. CD. The British Library, NSACD 111, 2012.
Bush, Kate. *Director's Cut*. CD. Fish People FPCD001, 2011.
Butterfield, Christopher and Kurt Schwitters. *Music For Klein And Beuys / Ursonate / Pillar Of Snails*. CD. Artifact ART 015, 1993.
Cage, John. *The 25-Year Retrospective Concert of the Music of John Cage*. CD. Wergo WER6247-2, 1994.

Carter, Betty. *Out There with Betty Carter*. LP. Peacock Records PLP 90, 1958.
Celentano, Adriano. *Nostalrock*. LP. Clan Celentano CLN 65764, 1973.
Chumbawamba. *ABCDEFG*. CD. No Masters / Westpark NMCD33 / WP87186, 2010.
Chopin, Henri. *Audiopoems*. CD. ? Records 05, 2001.
Chopin, Henri. *Le Corpsbis & Co*. CD. Nepless PS 961 1001, 1996.
Cobbing, Bob. *The Spoken Word*. CD. The British Library, NSACD 42, 2009.
Cohen, Leonard. *Live in London*. CD. Columbia 88697405022, 2009.
Crystal Castles. *Crystal Castles*. CD. Different DIFB 1200, 2008.
Cutler, Ivor. *Dandruff*. LP. Virgin OVED 33, 1974.
Cutler, Ivor [The Ivor Cutler Trio]. *Ludo*. CD. Rev-Ola CRREV3, 2002.
Cutler, Ivor. *Jammy Smears*. LP. Virgin OVED 12, 1976.
Cutler, Ivor. *Velvet Donkey*. LP. Virgin OVED 34, 1975.
Den Sorte Skole. *III*. LP. No label or catalogue no., 2013.
Den Sorte Skole. *Indians & Cowboys*. LP. No label or catalogue no., 2015.
Diddley, Bo. *Bo Diddley*. LP. Chess LP-1431, 1958.
D. J. Spooky That Subliminal Kid. *Rhythm Science: Excerpts and Allegories From The Sub Rosa Archives*. CD. Sub Rosa SR 201, 2004.
Dutton, Paul. *Mouth Pieces*. CD. OHM OHM/AVTR 021, 2000.
Dylan, Bob. *Blonde on Blonde*. LP. Columbia CS 9316/9317, 1966.
Dylan, Bob. *Bringing It All Back Home*. LP. Columbia CS 9128, 1965.
Dylan, Bob. *Highway 61 Revisited*. LP: Columbia CL 2389, 1965.
Ellis, Shirley. *The Complete Congress Recordings*. CD. Connoisseur Collection VSOP CD, 2001.
Eriksen, Tim. *Northern Roots Live in Náměšť*. CD. Indies Scope MAM451-2, 2009.
Fisher, Morgan. *Miniatures One & Two*. CD. Cherry Red, CDBRED361, 2008.
Gaillard, Slim. *The Extrovert Spirit of Slim Gaillard*. CD. Avid AMSC1141, 2014.
Galás, Diamanda. *Guilty Guilty Guilty*. CD. Mute CDSTUMM274, 2008.
Greif, Randy. *Alice in Wonderland*. CD. Soleilmoon SOL 55, 2010.
Gysin, Brion. *Self-Portrait Jumping*. CD. Made to Measure MTM 33, 1993.
Hancock, Butch. *Own & Own*. LP. Demon D-FIEND 150, 1989.
Hodeir, André. *Anna Luvia Plurabelle: A Jazz Cantata*. LP. Philips PHS 900-255, 1966.
James Joyce / Finnegans Wake. LP. Caedmon TC 1086, 1959.
Jeck, Philip. *An Ark for the Listener*. CD. Touch, 2010.
Jefferson, Eddie. *There I Go Again*. LP. Prestige P-24095, 1980.

Jesse Dangerously. *How to Express Your Dissenting Political Viewpoint Through Origami*. CD. Backburner Recordings HPK0006.
Kano. *Made in the Manor*. LP. Parlophone 082564 6484232, 2016.
King Pleasure and Annie Ross. *King Pleasure Sings, Annie Ross Sings*. LP. Prestige P7128, 1986.
Knížák, Milan. *Broken Music*. LP. Sub Rosa SR400, 2015.
Knížák, Milan. *Broken / Re/broken*. CD. Sub Rosa SR 409CD, 2015.
Lacy, Steve and Brion Gysin. *Songs*. CD. Hat Hut Hatology 625, 2006.
Lambert, Hendricks & Ross. *The Hottest New Group in Jazz*. LP. Columbia CL1403, 1960.
Lansky, Paul. *More Than Idle Chatter*. CD. Bridge BCD9050, 1994.
Lehrer, Tom. *More of Tom Lehrer*. LP. Decca LF 1323, 1959.
Little Richard. *All-Time Hits*. LP. Specialty SNTF 5000, 1969.
Lucier, Alvin. *I Am Sitting in a Room*. CD. Lovely Music LCD 1013, 1990.
Magma. *Theusz Hamtaahk – Trilogie*. CD. Seventh SRA 29-30-31, 2001.
Mantler, Michael. *Hide and Seek*. CD. ECM, ECM1738, 2001.
Mantler, Michael. *Silence*. LP. WATT Works / Virgin WATT/ 5, 1977.
Mantler, Michael and Edward Gorey. *The Hapless Child and Other Inscrutable Stories*. LP. WATT Works / Virgin WATT/4, 1976.
Marclay, Christian. *More Encores*. CD. ReR Megacorp ReR CM1, 1997.
Material. *The Road to the Western Lands*. LP. Triloka/Mercury 314558021-1, 1998.
Material. *Seven Souls*. CD. Triloka/Mercury 314534905-2, 1997.
Oswald, John. *Grayfolded*. CD. Swell/Snapper SMDCD 215, 1999.
Oswald, John. *prePlexure*. LP. Fony 82, 2014.
Oswald, John. *Plexure*. CD. Disk Union AVAN 016, 1993.
Oswald, John. *69/96*. CD. Seeland SEELAND 515, 2001.
Partch, Harry. *Enclosure Two: Harry Partch*. CD. Innova 401, 1995.
People Like Us. *Abridged Too Far*. LP. Discrepant CREP41, 2017.
Pickett, Wilson. *The Exciting Wilson Pickett*. LP. Atlantic SD 8129, 1966.
Redman, Dewey. *The Ear of the Behearer*. LP. Impulse! AS-9250, 1973.
Reed, Lou. *Transformer*. LP. RCA Victor LSP-4807, 1972.
Rivingtons, The. *The Liberty Years*. CD. EMI CDP-7-95204-2, 1991.
Scatman John. *Scatman's World*. CD. RCA 74321289942, 1995.
Schmidt, Martyn, ed. *Vocology #02: 'Dada Data Wrecking Ball'*. Digital streaming / download. Atemwerft AW 003/d, 2015.
Schwitters, Kurt and Jaap Blonk. *Ursonate*. CD. Basta 3091452, 2004.
Sigur Rós. *()*. LP. FatCat FATLP22 / [PIAS] PIASB122dlp, 2002.
Smiley Culture. 'Cockney Translation'. 12-inch single. Fashion Records FAD 020, 1984).

Spoonie Gee. 'Spoonin Rap' 12-inch. Sound Of New York QC 708, 1979.
Steele, Jan and John Cage. *Voices and Instruments*. LP. Obscure/Island, Obscure No. 5, 1976.
Stockhausen, Karlheinz. *Hymnen*. LP: Deutsche Grammophon 2707039, 1969.
Talking Heads. *Fear of Music*. LP. Sire 56707, 1979.
Trashmen, The. *Surfin' Bird*. CD. Sundazed SC 6064, 2010.
Trythall, Richard, Joseph Hudson and Randall McClellan. *Players And Tape*. LP. American Contemporary CRI SD 382, 1977.
Unwin, Stanley. *Rotatey Diskers with Unwin*. CD. Castle Pie PIESD289, 2002.
Various Artists. *A Complete Introduction To Sugar Hill Records*. CD. Universal / Sanctuary / Castle 2736484, 2010.
Various Artists. *An Anthology of Noise & Electronic Music: Seventh and Last A-Chronology 1930-2012*. CD. Sub Rosa SR300, 2013.
Various Artists. *Baku: Symphony of Sirens: Sound Experiments in the Russian Avant Garde*. CD. ReR Megacorp RER RAG 1&2, 2008.
Various Artists. *Carnivocal: A Celebration of Sound Poetry*. CD. Red Deer Press / Omikron Publishing, 1999.
Various Artists. *Doo Wop: The R&B Vocal Group Sound 1950-1960*. CD. Fantastic Voyage FVTD 129, 2011.
Various Artists. *Doo Wop: The Rock & Roll Vocal Group Sound 1957-1961*. CD. Fantastic Voyage FVTD 129, 2012.
Various Artists. *Doo Wop Revival: The R&B Vocal Group Sound 1961-1962*. CD. Fantastic Voyage FVTD 190, 2014.
Various Artists. *Great Googa Mooga!* CD. Ace CDCHD 880, 2003.
Various Artists. *Music from the Motion Picture O Brother, Where Art Thou?* CD. Mercury 170069-2, 2000.
Various Artists. *OU Sound Poetry: An Anthology*. LP. Alga Marghen plana-OU 15VocSon045, 2002.
Various Artists. *Songs the Bonzo Dog Band Taught Us*. LP. Flashback FB2LP1006, 2016.
Various Artists. *Waywords and Meansigns: Recreating Finnegans Wake [in its whole wholume]*. Online files. http://www.waywordsandmeansigns.com/.
Wildchild. 'Renegade Master' 12-inch. Hi Life Recordings 577131-1, 1995.
Wildchild. 'Renegade Master 98'. 12-inch. Hi Life Recordings 569 279-1, 1998.
Wyatt, Robert. *Rock Bottom*. CD. Hannibal HNCD 1426, 1998.
Wyatt, Robert. *Shleep*. LP. Domino REWIGLP45, 2008.
Yankovic, 'Weird Al'. *The Essential*. CD. Way Moby / Volcano / Legacy, 2009.

FILM, TELEVISION, RADIO AND PODCASTS

Alice. Directed by Jan Švankmajer, 1988.
Alice in Wonderland. Directed by Jonathan Miller, 1966.
Dont Look Back. Directed by D.A. Pennebaker, 1967
Gaga for Dada: The Original Art Rebels. Presented by Jim Moir. BBC TV (broadcast 21 September 2016).
Hip-Hop Evolution. Directed by Darby Wheeler, Sam Dunn and Scot McFadyen, 2016.
'The Joy of Gibberish', *Fry's English Delight*, Season 2, ep. 4. Audible download, 2010.
Radio Dada, presented by Alexei Sayle. BBC Radio 4 (broadcast 1 October 2016).
Slim Gaillard's Civilisation. Directed by Anthony Wall, 1989.
Vivian Stanshall: The Canyons of His Mind. BBC Four (broadcast, 11 June 2004).

INDEX

ABC in Sound (Cobbing) 50–1
absurdity 12, 19, 40, 70, 78
A.D.O.R. 64–5
Aerosmith 94
Alice books (*Alice's Adventures in Wonderland*, *Alice Through the Looking-Glass*) 1, 9, 10, 19, 24, 26–8, 32, 33, 38, 43, 69, 71, 73, 99
  audio adaptation 38–40, 41–2
  film adaptation 40–1, 69
Alice in Wonderland (Greif) 41–2
Alice in Wonderland (Miller) 40–1
'Alifib/Alife' (Wyatt) 77
alphabets 29–31, 50–1, 76, 85
Anderson, Laurie 33, 116 n.29
animals 17–18, 24–8, 30, 41, 80, 109 n.42
Anna Livia Plurabelle (Hodeir) 44, 113 n.50
Appel, Nadav 78–9, 86–7
'Aria' (Cage) 58
Armstrong, Louis 61, 81–2
Artaud, Antonin 10, 103
Artman, Deborah 62
audiobooks 39–40, 41, 71
Avalanches, The 66, 119 n.62
'A was once an apple pie' (Lear) 29–30

babble 9, 10, 16, 25, 32, 34, 40, 55, 62, 94
backing vocals 70, 87, 90–1, 93, 125 n.60, *see also* doo-wop; non-lexical vocals
Bakhtin, Mikhail 18, 60
Ball, Hugo 2, 5, 48–9, 56, 57, 60, 65, 71–2
Ball, Patrick 43
'Ballad of a Thin Man' (Dylan) 72–3, 121 n.17
beatboxing 92–3, 111 n.39, 126 n.66
Beatles, The 69–70, 79
'Be-Bop-a-Lula' 4, 90
Beckett, Samuel 12, 40, 56, 73, 77
Bellos, David 18–19
Berio, Luciano 44, 55–6, 58, 118 n.55
'Beyond Doo-Wop or How I Came to Realize that Hank Williams is Avant-Garde' (Dutton) 91–2
beyonsense, *see* zaum
'Bird's the Word, The' (Rivingtons) 88–9
Björk 52, 79, 92
Blind Blake 125 n.58
Blonk, Jaap 20–1, 46, 49, 53–4, 56, 72, 92, 101, 128 n.6
'Blue Moon' 86, 87, 93
'Blues in Bob Minor' (Wyatt) 75–6
'Bob' (Yankovic) 75
Bo Dudley (Dudley Moore) 90, 124 n.58

INDEX

body 18, 50, 51–3, 54, 62, 80, 97, *see also* dance
Bök, Christian 49, 92–3, 115 n.16
Bonzo Dog Doo-Dah Band 69–70
Bowie, David 61
Broken Music (Knižak) 61
Buckley, Tim 96–7
Burroughs, William 5, 10, 49, 60–1, 63, 76, 96, 119 n.61
Bush, Kate 44
Busy Bee 93, 126 n.67
Byrds, The 69
Byrne, David 5

Cage, John 35, 43–4, 58, 60, 77
Campbell, Joseph 36, 74
'Canyons of Your Mind' (Bonzo Dog Doo-Dah Band) 70
carnivalesque 18, 70
Carroll, Lewis 1–2, 5, 8, 10, 12, 23, 25–8, 32, 38–42, 56, 69, 74, 76, 99, 102–3
Carter, Betty 81–2
Celentano, Adriano 18
Chandra, Sheila 52
Chopin, Henri 49–50, 53, 55, 57, 65, 77
Chumbawamba 20, 72
Cleverdon, Douglas 39–40, 117 n.45
Cobain, Kurt 61, 122 n.22
Cobbing, Bob 5, 49–52, 55, 56, 59–60, 76, 77, 92
'Cockadoodledon't' (Cutler) 18
'Cockney Translation' (Smiley Culture) 94
Cocteau Twins, The 96–7
code 3, 12, 36–7, 71, 78, 82, 86–7, 91, 94, 100, 123 n.46
Cohen, Leonard 90–1
Coltrane, John 69, 96, 97
Connor, Steven 35, 37–8, 112 n.47
country music 5, 91–2

Crazy Frog 21, 101
Crystal Castles 44
'Cucurrucucú Paloma' 18
Cutler, Ivor 5, 18, 69, 71, 77, 120 n.10
cut-up 5, 12, 58, 60–1, 72

Dada 2, 21, 46, 48–9, 53, 57, 58, 65, 68, 69, 71–2, 76, 82, 91, 103, 107 n.17, 121 n.21
dance 29, 55, 61, 64–5, 80, 88, 93, *see also* body
délire 10–11, 36, 103
Den Sorte Skole 66, 119 n.62
'Desolation Row' (Dylan) 74
'Diddie Wah Diddie' 125 n.58
Disney 101
Dolar, Mladen 105 n.2
doo-wop 2, 3, 5, 69, 85–8, 91–2, 93, 96
dub 34, 64, 119 n.61
'Duchess, The' (Wyatt) 76
Dufrêne, François 49, 56
Dutton, Paul 5, 53, 91–2, 125 n.63
Dylan, Bob 12, 68, 72–6

Ebbinghaus, Hermann 72, 86, 120 n.13
'Ebonics' (Big L) 94
Eco, Umberto 19
Edsels, The 4, 87
Eklips 93, 123 n.66
'Elements, The' (Lehrer) 100, 127 n.2
Eliot, T.S. 14, 26, 33, 58, 74
Ellis Shirley 85
Eno, Brian 71
Eriksen, Tim 53

Fatboy Slim 64–5
Finnegans Wake (Joyce) 34, 35–7, 38, 42–4, 60, 74, 77
Fisher, Morgan 77

INDEX

Flescher, Jacqueline 9, 29
folklore 13, 48–9, 107 n.17
folk music 35, 53, 72, 74, 101
foreign language 13, 15–16, 18–20, 45, 56–7, 83, 94, 95–6
Fry, Stephen 10, 71, 90, 91, 100, 107 n.17
Furman, Ezra 91
futurism 2, 46–9, 58, 68, 72, 80

Gaillard, Slim 81–3, 95
Gál, Bernhard 57
Galás, Diamanda 52, 53, 79, 92
Gargantua (Rabelais) 19
Gashlycrumb Tinies, The (Gorey) 30
gibberish 8, 9, 10–11, 18–19, 45, 50–1, 52, 56–7, 88, 90, 94, 96–7, 101
Gillespie, Dizzy 81, 82, 83
Giorno, John 60, 67, 92, 116 n.29
glitch 3, 12, 35, 61, 110 n.25
gobbledygook 9, 12, 56
Goons, The 12, 69
Gorey, Edward 27, 30, 77
Grandmaster Caz 93–4
Grandmaster Flash 118–19 n.60
grasping after sense 3, 13, 15–16, 20, 42–3, 55, *see also* nonsense moment
Grateful Dead 64
Grayfolded (Oswald) 64
Great Googa Mooga (album) 79–80
Greif, Randy 41–2, 100
Gysin, Brion 2, 5, 49, 58–61, 63, 77, 117 n.45

Hampton the Hampster 21
Hancock, Butch 84–5
Hausmann, Raoul 48, 49
Hayden, Ethan 96, 107 n.17

'Heebie Jeebies' (Armstrong) 81–2
Hendricks, Jon 82
Heyman, Michael 8, 11, 14–15, 16, 19
hip-hop 2, 12, 64, 93–4, 95, 126 n.66
Hodeir, André 44, 113 n.50
homophones 15, 37–8, 57
'Honki Ponki' 128 n.4
Hopelandic (*Vonlenska*) 96
Hughes, David 72, 83
Humpty Dumpty 18, 23, 74

I Am Sitting in a Room (Lucier) 54–5, 56, 65
'I Am That I Am' (Gysin) 59
'Idle Chatter' (Lansky) 55
'I Don't Work You Dig' (Gysin) 59
Ihde, Don 3, 18
imitation 4, 17–18, 26, 45, 57, 82, 86, 93
'Incantation by Laughter' (Khlebnikov) 47, 114 n.7
'I Zimbra' (Talking Heads) 71

'Jabberwocky' (Carroll) 23, 25–6, 33, 43, 56, 127 n.2
Jakobson, Roman 20, 47, 114 n.7
Jandl, Ernst 57
jargon 9, 12, 56
jazz 12, 44, 52, 59, 69, 76, 77–8, 82–3, 95–6
Jeck, Philip 110 n.25
Jefferson, Eddie 82
Jefferson Airplane 69
Jesse Dangerously 100, 127 n.2
Johnson, Jeri 32–3, 34
Joyce, James 1, 2, 10, 31–8, 42–4, 56, 58, 60, 74, 77, 82

Kahn, Douglas 15–16
Kano 95
Kenner, Hugh 34

Khlebnikov, Velimir 17, 47–8
King Pleasure 82
Kittler, Friedrich 120 n.13
Knižak, Milan 61
Kobaïan 95–6
Kruchenykh, Alexei 17, 47–8, 114 n.7
LaBelle, Brandon 46, 52, 78
'Labio Dental Fricative' (Stanshall) 70–1
'La Catorra Criolla' (Conde) 94
'Land of 1000 Dances' (Pickett) 80
language, *see* foreign language; language acquisition; nonsense
language acquisition 14–15, 18–19, 86, 120 n.13
Lansky, Paul 33, 55
Las Ketchup 21, 101
Lear, Edward 1, 2, 5, 10, 14, 24–5, 26–31, 33, 69, 70, 76, 85, 96, 100, 102
Lecercle, Jean-Jacques 8, 10, 11, 23, 24, 25–6, 34, 36, 56, 74, 102–3
'Le Corps' (Chopin) 50
Lehrer, Tom 100, 127 n.2
liberature 38, 80
limericks 29, 30
listening 3, 5, 15–16, 20, 23, 24–5, 28, 31–2, 34–5, 42–3, 54–5, 63, 65, 100, *see also* grasping after sense
lists 21, 29–30, 53–4, 100, 127 n.2
literature and sound 2, 23–44, 68
Little Richard 5, 79, 80, 88, 92
logatomes 72, 86–7, 92, 99
logorrhoea 10, 19
Lost Objects (Bang on a Can) 62
Lucier, Alvin 33, 54–5, 56, 65
lyrics 18, 64–5, 70, 75–6, 80, 81–2, 90–1, 93–6
 misheard 16, 90

McCaffery, Steve 46, 60, 92
McKenna, Terence 74–5
McLean, Don 122 n.22
Magma 95–6
Mahy, Margaret 80
Malcolm, Noel 8–9, 11, 45, 100
'Man from the Land of Fandango, The' (Mahy) 80
Mann, Barry 87–8, 90–1
Marcels, The 86, 87, 92, 93
Marclay, Christian 5, 35, 61–2, 66
Marinetti, Filippo Tommaso 46–7, 48, 72
Marshall, Wayne 95
mash-up 66, 94, 88, 100, 101
Maslen, Robert 8, 23
Material 119 n.61
Melly, George 20, 72, 77
Miller, Jonathan 40–1, 69
Milligan, Spike 69, 76
Miniatures (Fisher) 77
Moir, Jim (Vic Reeves) 107 n.17
More Encores (Marclay) 61–2
Morgenstern, Christian 96, 120 n.13
morpheme 47, 50, 64, 84, 99
Morrison, Van 44, 63, 82, 83, 112 n.47
Morton Robinson, Henry 36, 74
mouth 20, 30, 31–2, 37, 46, 52, 59, 78, 91, 100
museme 63, 64, 118 n.59
music 1, 2, 3–4, 11, 12, 13, 16, 17–18, 19–20, 25–6, 28–9, 32–4, 42–3, 42–4, 46, 53–6, 61–2, 63–5, 67–98
'Muzikaret' (Braaxtaal) 53–4
'My Pink Half of the Drainpipe' (Bonzo Dog Doo-Dah Band) 70

'Name Game, The' (Ellis) 85
Nancy, Jean-Luc 16

Něco z Alenky (Švankmajer) 41
'New Banger' (Kano) 95
Nichol, bp (Barrie Phillip) 53, 60, 76
non-lexical vocals 83–5, 90–1, 93–4, *see also* backing vocals; beatboxing; doo-wop; scat; vocalese; yodel
no-nonsense 39–40, 41, 71, 73, 100, 128 n.6
non-semantic voicing, *see* semantic voicing
nonsense, *see also* babble; gibberish; jargon; nonsense literature; nonsense moment
 definitions 7–12
 language 9, 11, 16, 45, 57, 83, 90, 126 n.66
 logic 1, 8, 9, 10, 12, 24, 27, 29, 30, 33, 40, 57, 61, 75, 88, 94, 102
 synonyms 9
 typology 12
 used as criticism 8, 9–10
 used as strategy 8, 10, 30, 70, 97
 vitality 4, 68, 80, 87, 103, 126 n.67
nonsense alphabets 29–30, 50–1, 76, 85
nonsense literature 1, 2, 3–4, 7, 9, 10–11, 14, 23–31, 39–42, 80, 97, 99, 102–3
nonsense moment 2–3, 12, 13, 15–16, 20, 21, 45, 55, 91, 102, 103, *see also* grasping after sense

'O Death' 53
'oslo solo' (Cobbing) 60
Oswald, John 5, 35, 63–4, 66

palimpsest (sonic) 2, 32, 56, 93, 94
'Papa-Oom-Mow-Mow' (Rivingtons) 88–9

Paris, Nicole 93, 123 n.66
parole in libertà 46, 80
Parsons, Marnie 1, 16, 18, 47–8, 73, 76, 83–4, 105 n.2, 107 n.17
Partch, Harry 44
patois 94–5, *see also* slang
P. Diddy (Sean Combs, Puff Daddy) 125 n.58
Peake, Mervyn 8, 23, 27, 76
Peel, John 71
Penman, Ian 96–7
People Like Us 66, 119 n.62
Perloff, Nancy 47, 114 n.7
permutation 12, 58–60, 61, 64–5
permutation poem 58–60, 61, 117 n.45
phoneme 15, 25, 31, 37, 42, 47, 50, 57, 60, 63, 64–5, 77, 84, 99, 103
phonography 14, 25, 34–5, 37
phonology 18, 25–6, 23, 31, 42, 55, 94, 103
Pickett, Wilson 80
Pitilli, Lawrence 86–7
Plexure (Oswald) 63
plunderphonics 5, 46, 58, 63–4, 119 n.61
populism 13–14, 97–8, 103
'Prisencolinensinainciusol' (Celentano) 18

'Quien Puso El Bomp' (Teen Tops) 88

Rabelais, François 10, 19, 38, 127 n.1
rap 13, 64–5, 93–4, 95, 125 n.58, 126 n.66
'Rapper's Delight' (Sugarhill Gang) 93–4
'Rapper's Deutsch' (G.L.S.-United) 94

'Ratatatay'
  (Chumbawamba) 20, 72
Redman, Dewey 120 n.5
Reed, Lou 96
reggae 94–5
remix 13, 21, 35, 44, 46, 57, 61,
  62–6, 100, 101–2, 118–19
  n.60, 119 n.61
'Renegade Master'
  (Wildchild) 64–5
rhyme 5, 18–19, 23, 29–31, 32,
  43, 57, 76–7, 79–80
rhythm 8, 9, 16, 23, 29–31, 33,
  36, 42, 51–2, 54–5, 60,
  64–5, 75, 77, 79–80, 81, 93
Ríos, Julián 10, 34, 37–8, 80,
  111 n.33
Rivingtons, The 86, 88–9,
  121 n.17
Ross, Annie 82
Roubaud, Jacques 67
'Rouge' (Chopin) 50, 65
Run-DMC 94
Russolo, Luigi 46–7, 58, 72

sampling 13, 35, 41–2, 58, 62–6,
  71, 93, 119 n.62
Sayle, Alexei 107 n.17
scat 2, 3–4, 13, 20–1, 76, 77,
  81–2, 84, 85, 93, 96, 99, 101
Scatman John (John Paul
  Larkin) 20–1, 101
Schwitters, Kurt 20–1, 48–9, 71,
  72, 92, 96, 101
'Scroobius Pip, The' (Lear) 24–6
semantics 12, 13, 15, 16, 18,
  25–6, 33, 43, 46, 50, 53, 60,
  62, 64–5, 75, 77, 81, 82, 84,
  85, 87–8, 91, 94, 96–7, 99
semantic voicing 3, 13, 53, 81,
  84, 85, 96–7, 99
sense, *see* grasping after sense;
  nonsense; nonsense
  moment; semantics, syntax

Sewell, Elizabeth 7–8, 18, 26–7
Shankar, Ravi 41, 69
Shleep (Wyatt) 76
Sigur Rós 79, 96, 107 n.17
Sinfonia (Berio) 55–6
slang 12, 87, 90, 94–5, 100,
  124 n.58
'Slang Like This' 94–5
social media 19–21, 66, 101
song 2, 12, 13, 16, 18, 20, 29,
  34, 44, 50, 52–3, 54–5, 64,
  67–98, 99, 101
sonorous envelope 13
sound poetry 1, 5, 11, 13, 14,
  45–53, 55, 56–7, 58, 66, 67,
  76, 92, 102, 107 n.17
sound recording 15, 34–5, 38–44,
  46, 49–51, 54, 58, 59, 61–4,
  112 n.45
sound/sense distinction 1, 3,
  12–17, 33, 46, 48, 62, 99
speech music 53–6, *see also* non-
  lexical vocals
Spoonie Gee 64–5
Stanley, Ralph 53
Stanshall, Vivian 70–1, 100
Stein, Gertrude 9, 10
Stereolab 96
Sterne, Laurence 10, 102, 111 n.33
Stewart, Susan 12–13, 13–14,
  79–80, 107 n.17
Stockhausen, Karlheinz 56, 58
'Subterranean Homesick Blues'
  (Dylan) 75
'Sumer Is Icumen In' 18
'Surfin' Bird' (Trashmen) 88–9
surrealism 2, 34, 38, 41, 69–70,
  72, 74–5, 82, 93
Švankmajer, Jan 41
syntax 4, 12, 16, 25, 47, 60

Talking Heads 71–2
tape 46, 49–53, 54–5, 58, 59, 60,
  77, 115 n.17

INDEX

tape loops 13, 14, 59, 65, 66, 77
technology 14, 34–5, 59, 61–2, 93, 120 n.13
'Thema (Omaggio a Joyce)' (Berio) 44, 118 n.55
Thunderthighs 125 n.60
Tigges, Wim 7, 107 n.17
'Tower of Song' (Cohen) 90
translation 18–19, 25, 47–8, 57, 94
Trashmen, The 88–9
Trythall, Richard 118 n.55
'Tutti Frutti' (Little Richard) 79, 80, 88

Ulysses (Joyce) 31–5, 37, 44
Unwin, Stanley 25, 43, 100–1
Ursonate (Schwitters) 20–1, 49, 71, 72, 77, 101
Utter Zoo, The (Gorey) 30

'Vain Cock' ('Poda Kapala') 18
Vander, Christian 95–6
van Rooten, Luis 18, 57
Vincent, Gene 4, 79
vocables 3, 13, 15, 36, 81, 83–4, 90
vocalese 2, 3–4, 13, 44, 82, 85, 93, 96, 99
voice 11, 14, 17, 25, 31, 32–8, 39, 44, 49–53, 54–5, 57, 60, 62, 63, 71, 78–95, *see also* non-lexical vocals

Voices of Babel // Babel of Voices (Atemwerft) 57
Vout-o-Reenee 83

'Walk on the Wild Side' (Reed) 90
'Walk this Way' (Run-DMC, Aerosmith) 94
Watson, Leo 81, 82
Watts, Reggie 93, 126 n.66
'West Texas Waltz' (Hancock) 84–5
'Who Put the Bomp (in the Bomp Bomp Bomp)' (Mann) 87–8, 90
Wildchild 64–5
'Williams Mix' (Cage) 58
'Wonderful Widow of Eighteen Springs, The' 44, 77
Wyatt, Robert 71, 75–8

Yankovic, 'Weird Al' 75, 122 n.22
yodel 2, 84–5, 92, 99, 101
yodeleme 84, 92, 99

Zang Tumb Tumb (Marinetti) 47, 72
zaum 17, 48–9, 101, 114 n.7
Zukofsky, Louis 76, 83–4
'Zungguzungguguzungguzeng' (Yellowman) 95

www.ingramcontent.com/pod-product-compliance
Lightning Source LLC
Chambersburg PA
CBHW070733230426
43665CB00016B/2227